Exploring
America
in the **1960s**

Exploring America in the 1960s

Grades 6–8

Our Voices Will Be Heard

Molly Sandling &
Kimberley L. Chandler, Ph.D.

The College of William and Mary
School of Education
Center for Gifted Education
P.O. Box 8795
Williamsburg, VA 23187

Edited by Rachel Taliaferro

Production design by Raquel Trevino

ISBN-13: 978-1-61821-109-5

Prufrock Press Inc.
P.O. Box 8813
Waco, TX 76714-8813
Phone: (800) 998-2208
Fax: (800) 240-0333
http://www.prufrock.com

Contents

Acknowledgement

Thanks to Pamela N. Harris, who acted as the
editorial assistant for this unit.

Unit Overview

Introduction to the *Exploring America* Units

These humanities units will focus on the way in which the literature, art, and music of each decade reflect the history and events that were occurring in America at that time. These units are intended to stimulate student interest and creativity, to develop higher order thinking skills, and to promote interdisciplinary learning.

The units could be used as a supplement to a social studies curriculum or a language arts curriculum, or could be used as stand-alone materials in a gifted education program.

Introduction to *Exploring America in the 1960s: Our Voices Will Be Heard*

Exploring America in the 1960s: Our Voices Will Be Heard is a unit that starts with the hope of the early 1960s as seen in John F. Kennedy's Camelot, moving to the increasing disillusionment and despair by the end of the decade as those hopes were dashed by assassinations and the involvement in Vietnam. Topics included in the unit are:

  » the hope and promise of the early 1960s as seen in the Kennedy administration and the popular music of the early Beatles and Beach Boys;
  » reactions to popular culture as seen in Andy Warhol and Pop Art;
  » the 1963 March on Washington;

» music and literature that reveals the discontent and demands of other groups such as environmentalists, women, and the counterculture;

» Vietnam protests and the changing view of our government and our role in the world;

» the frustration with the lack of movement in civil rights, the split of the Civil Rights Movement and the progress of Black musicians through Motown; and

» the desire to escape the friction and tension of the 1960s and yearning for a simpler life with Woodstock by the end of the decade.

Standards Alignment

Social Studies

This unit includes activities that address the National Council for the Social Studies (NCSS) National Curriculum Standards for Social Studies. Specifically, the activities relate to 10 themes of the National Curriculum Standards for Social Studies: Culture; Time, Continuity, and Change; People, Places, and Environments; Individual Development and Identity; Individuals, Groups, and Institutions; Power, Authority, and Governance; Production, Distribution, and Consumption; Science, Technology, and Society; Global Connections; and Civic Ideals and Practices.

English/Language Arts

This unit also includes activities that align to these Anchor Standards of the Common Core State Standards in English Language Arts (CCSS-ELA):

» CCSS.ELA-Literacy.CCRA.R.1 Read closely to determine what the text says explicitly and to make logical inferences from it; cite specific textual evidence when writing or speaking to support conclusions drawn from the text.

» CCSS.ELA-Literacy.CCRA.R.2 Determine central ideas or themes of a text and analyze their development; summarize the key supporting details and ideas.

» CCSS.ELA-Literacy.CCRA.R.4 Interpret words and phrases as they are used in a text, including determining technical, connotative, and figurative meanings, and analyze how specific word choices shape meaning or tone.

» CCSS.ELA-Literacy.CCRA.R.7 Integrate and evaluate content presented in diverse media and formats, including visually and quantitatively, as well as in words.

» CCSS.ELA-Literacy.CCRA.R.9 Analyze how two or more texts address similar themes or topics in order to build knowledge or to compare the approaches the authors take.

» CCSS.ELA-Literacy.CCRA.R.10 Read and comprehend complex literary and informational texts independently and proficiently.

Overarching Concept

The overarching concept for this unit is *identity*. This concept can help students to understand events, music, art, and literature during the 1960s. The unit explores the decade, giving students multiple opportunities to analyze events based on a developing understanding of how the idea of identity applies to specific situations. The conceptual approach also allows students the opportunity to make comparisons to other time periods, thus developing a deeper understanding of the generalizations about identity and when they may or may not apply.

The first lesson in this unit introduces the concept of identity. Teachers may wish to conduct an activity based on Hilda Taba's (1962) Concept Development Model prior to teaching the first lesson. Students are asked to brainstorm examples of identity, categorize their examples, identify "nonexamples" of the concept, and make generalizations about the concept. The following generalizations about *identity* are incorporated into this unit of study:

>> Identity changes with new ideas, experiences, conditions, or in response to other expressions of identity.

>> Identity is created, either by a group or person or by outsiders, and self-created identities may be different from how others see one's self.

>> There are multiple elements of identity and at different times, different elements have greater or lesser importance.

>> Although members of a group or society may have different individual identities, they still share particular elements of identity.

Identity is integrated throughout unit lessons and deepens students' understanding of social studies and a given historical period. Students examine the relationship of important ideas, abstractions, and issues through the application of the concept "generalizations."

Curriculum Framework

Concept Goal

Goal 1: To understand the concept of identity in 1960s America.
Students will be able to:

>> describe how the American identity changed during the 1960s, and

>> describe how changes in American identity in the 1960s are revealed in the music, art, and literature of the decade.

Process Goals

Goal 2: To develop skills in historical analysis and song and artwork interpretation. Students will be able to:

>> define the context in which a song or piece of art was produced and the implications of context for understanding the artifact;

>> describe a writer's or artist's intent in producing a given song or piece of art based on understanding of text and context;

>> consider short- and long-term consequences of a given document or artifact; and

>> analyze the effects of given documents or artifacts on the interpretation of historical events.

Goal 3: To develop analytical and interpretive skills in literature. Students will be able to:
- » describe what a selected literary passage means,
- » cite similarities and differences in meaning among selected works of literature, and
- » make inferences based on information in given passages.

Content Goal

Goal 4: To develop an understanding of historical events occurring in the United States during the 1960s. Students will be able to:
- » describe major historical events during the 1960s that affected the American identity, and
- » describe music, art, and literature of the 1960s that reflected the American identity.

Assessing Student Learning

For formative assessments, teachers should evaluate student progress based on the quality of individual products and achievement toward the goals of the unit. Question responses should be assessed based on demonstration of insight and ability to use text to support inferences. Writing activities should be assessed based on understanding of the social studies content, and may also be assessed for clarity and insight as desired. Oral presentations of completed work should be assessed based on coherence, content, and clarity of the presentation. Teachers may provide rubrics for students related to the required assignments or work with students to develop rubrics for assessment.

The culminating project for the unit, the "1960s Pop Art Project," will provide a comprehensive summative assessment that evaluates student learning about all four unit goals. Based on their study of the 1960s, students are to use a grid (like in some of Andy Warhol's paintings) in which they will include nine, 12, or 16 images that demonstrate important or defining events, people, or experiences that shaped American identity or values in the decade. This will give students the opportunity to study additional figures beyond those included in the unit.

Teaching Resources

Recommended History Textbooks

These are history textbooks that are recommended for providing supplementary information about the historical background of the events described in this unit.

Appleby, J. (2010). *American vision.* New York, NY: Glencoe/McGraw Hill.

Cayton, A. R. L., Perry, E. I., Reed, L., & Winkler, A. M. (2002). *Pathways to the present.* Upper Saddle River, NJ: Pearson Prentice Hall.

Davidson, J. W., Stoff, M. B., & Viola, H. J. (2002). *The American nation.* Upper Saddle River, NJ: Pearson Prentice Hall.

Kennedy, D. M., & Cohen, L. (2012). *American pageant.* Boston, MA: Cengage Learning.

Recommended Websites

» American Experience: *Eyes on the* Prize:
  http://www.pbs.org/wgbh/amex/eyesontheprize

» Earth Day Network:
  http://edu.earthday.org

» Internet Archive Movie Archive:
  http://archive.org/details/movies

» John F. Kennedy Presidential Library and Museum
  http://www.jfklibrary.org

» Library of Congress Civil Rights Themed Resources:
  http://www.loc.gov/teachers/classroommaterials/themes/civil-rights

» Library of Congress Song and Poetry Analysis Tools:
  http://www.loc.gov/teachers/lyrical/tools

» Lichtenstein Foundation:
  http://www.lichtensteinfoundation.org

» Martin Luther King, Jr. Research and Education Institute:
  http://mlk-kpp01.stanford.edu/index.php/resources/categories/C39

» National First Ladies' Library
  http://www.firstladies.org

» National Humanities Center
  http://nationalhumanitiescenter.org

» National Park Service, Historic Places of the Civil Rights Movement:
  http://www.cr.nps.gov/nr/travel/civilrights

» PBS History Detectives
  http://www.pbs.org/opb/historydetectives

» PBS Learning Media, Civil Rights Special Collection:
  http://www.teachersdomain.org/special/civil

» PBS Makers: Women Who Make America:
  http://www.pbs.org/makers/home

» PBS *Vietnam Passage: Journeys from War to Peace*
  http://www.pbs.org/vietnampassage/index.html

» Rock and Roll Hall of Fame Education Resources:
  http://www.rockhall.com/education

» Sixties Project Primary Document Archive:
  http://www2.iath.virginia.edu/sixties/HTML_docs/Resources/Primary.html

» Smithsonian Folkways:
  http://www.folkways.si.edu

Implementation Guide

This guide assists the teacher in implementing this unit in his or her classroom. It also includes background information about the instructional models utilized throughout the unit.

Guidelines

The following pages offer some general suggestions to help the teacher implement the unit effectively.

Support for Teachers Implementing the Unit

It is important for teachers implementing this unit to read it in depth before beginning instruction. Conferences and training workshops sponsored through the Center for Gifted Education (CFGE) can help teachers understand the core components of the unit and provide informal tips for teaching it. Customized professional development, including comprehensive curriculum planning for incorporating this humanities series, is also available. Please contact the CFGE at cfgepd@wm.edu for information about professional development options.

Suggested Grade Levels

Exploring America in the 1960s was designed for use with high-ability students in grades 6–8. Although the unit was developed for middle school students, some components may work well with students at other grade levels. Caution should be exercised when using the materials with elementary-aged students, however, as some of the music and literature contains mature themes.

How to Incorporate the Unit Within the Existing Social Studies Curriculum

This unit is intended to represent 5–8 weeks of instruction in social studies for high-ability learners. The unit may be taught as core content, or it may be used as a supplement to the core curriculum. The unit is also appropriate for use in a seminar setting.

Implementation Time

In this unit, a lesson is defined as at least two 2-hour sessions. A minimum of 40 instructional hours should be allocated for teaching the entire unit. Teachers are encouraged to extend the amount of time spent on the various topics included in the book based on available time and student interest.

Materials

Availability of materials. Given that this unit focuses on the 1960s decade, the materials are contemporary in nature and have not yet become part of the public domain. In most cases, it is suggested that teachers make use of Internet resources whenever possible rather than purchasing the materials cited. Both Prufrock Press and the Center for Gifted Education have developed websites that include a list of resources and their respective URLs: http://www.prufrock.com/Assets/ClientPages/exploring1960.aspx and http://education.wm.edu/centers/cfge/1960s. Because URLs tend to change, these websites will be updated periodically.

Potentially controversial materials. This unit focuses on the trends and issues in 1960s America. Some topics being discussed and some of the materials being used may be controversial to some students and parents. It is crucial that teachers preview all materials prior to teaching the unit and determine what is appropriate for their own schools and classrooms.

Teachers should always read the literature selections or listen to the musical selections before assigning them to students and be aware of what the school and/or district policy is on the use of materials that may be deemed controversial. Although many gifted readers are able to read books at a significantly higher Lexile level than what other children their age are reading, content that is targeted at older audiences may not be appropriate for them.

Text/Song/Artwork

- ☐ Made original, insightful contribution(s) to discussion?
- ☐ Extended or elaborated on a classmate's ideas?
- ☐ Used evidence from the text or another student's comments to support ideas?
- ☐ Synthesized information from discussion in a meaningful way?
- ☐ Posed questions that enhanced the discussion and led to more in-depth understanding?

Student comments: _____

_____

_____

Teacher comments: _____

_____

_____

Figure 1. Participation Checklist. Adapted from Center for Gifted Education (2011).

Assessment

This unit includes both formative and summative assessments, which are found at the end of each lesson plan. Because discussion plays a prominent role in the students' learning in this unit, teachers may want to consider teaching students a specific process for the discussion elements and develop tools for assessing student participation. The Socratic Seminar is one method for organizing discussions. (See http://socraticseminars.com/socratic-seminars/ or http://www.readwritethink.org/professional-development/strategy-guides/socratic-seminars-30600.html for additional information.) Or, the teacher may want to design a checklist, such as the one in Figure 1, to give to students to keep track of their contributions during discussions. The students can check off the criteria as they meet them. Using this checklist, the student and teacher can monitor the student's participation in various discussions.

Teaching Models

There are five teaching models that are used in the unit to facilitate student achievement toward the unit objectives. Teachers should familiarize themselves with these models before beginning the unit.

The models are designed to promote discussions in various settings. The teacher should determine the best way of organizing students for discussion in order to facilitate student understanding and appreciation for the variety of answers that are given. These teaching models also provide students with the opportunity to support their responses with evidence from the literature or other resources. Multiple perspectives can be shared and encouraged through appropriate use of the models. The models also may be used to prepare students for a discussion in another content area or about a current event. Students can complete the models in a whole group, in small groups, or individually before or as they engage in a discussion. Varying the group size and group composition will provide students with many perspectives for consideration. For more information, see Center for Gifted Education (2011).

The models are listed below and described in the pages that follow.

1. Identity Chart
2. Literature Analysis Model
3. Primary Source Document Analysis Model
4. Music Analysis Model
5. Art Analysis Model

Identity Chart

The Identity Chart (see Figure 2) allows students to consider the concept of identity as they study the events of the mid-20th century and examine the effect of those events on the American identity. Some scholars (Huntington, 2004; Smith, 2010) have defined the elements that comprise identity; for purposes of this unit, these include:

- » time and place,
- » history and myths,
- » culture and traditions,
- » race and ethnicity,
- » civic identity,
- » international role, and
- » economy.

Prior to the first lesson, you may have students develop a list of the elements that they believe are part of the American identity, and then compare it to the one listed here. Have students determine the definition of each element and give examples.

Tell students that in this unit, they will be examining the American identity in the 1960s, trying to get a better understanding of why Americans interacted as they did. Explain that identity is important because it shapes our actions and interactions with others. Have students answer the following questions on their own, then debrief in the large group:

- » Do all of the elements of identity that we listed affect your actions equally at all times? Explain your answer.
- » Sometimes various elements of identity are emphasized more than others. What are some examples? Why does this happen?
- » When is each of these elements most important? Least important? Why?
- » Which elements are most influential on your actions when you are at school? When you go on vacation? When you meet someone new? When you have to make an important decision? Why?

Explain that the questions and responses just discussed address individual (personal) identity. Have students answer the following questions:

- » What other types of identity are there?
- » How can a group's identity be different from an individual's identity within that group?

HANDOUT

Identity Chart

Identity	Time and Place
	Culture and Traditions
	History and Myths
	International Role
	Economy
	Civic Identity
	Race/Ethnicity

Figure 2. Identity Chart.

This discussion serves as the initial one regarding identity, specifically the American identity in the 1960s. Other unit activities will reinforce this concept. Teachers should revisit the identity generalizations regularly throughout the unit and make specific connections to the 1960s.

Literature Analysis Model

The Literature Analysis Model (see Figure 3) encourages students to consider seven aspects of a selection they are reading: key words, tone, mood, imagery, symbolism, key ideas, and the structure of writing (Center for Gifted Education, 2011; McKeague, 2009; National Governors Association Center for Best Practices & Council of Chief State School Officers, 2010). After reading a selection, this model helps students to organize their initial responses and provides them with a basis for discussing the piece in small or large groups. Whenever possible, students should be allowed to underline and make notes as they read the material. After marking the text, they can organize their notes into the model.

Suggested questions for completing and discussing the model are:

HANDOUT

Literature Analysis Model

Chosen or assigned text: _____	
Key words:	
Important ideas:	
Tone:	
Mood:	
Imagery:	
Symbolism:	
Structure of writing:	

Figure 3. Literature Analysis Model.

1. **Key words:** What words are important for understanding the selection? Which words did the author use for emphasis?
2. **Important ideas:** What is the main idea of the selection? What are other important ideas in the selection?
3. **Tone:** What is the attitude or what are the feelings of the author toward the subject of the selection? What words does the author use to indicate tone?
4. **Mood:** What emotions do you feel when reading the selection? How do the setting, images, objects, and details contribute to the mood?
5. **Imagery:** What are examples of the descriptive language that is used to create sensory impressions in the selection?
6. **Symbolism:** What symbols are used to represent other things?
7. **Structure of writing:** What are some important characteristics of the way this piece is written? How do the parts of this selection fit together and relate to each other? How do structural elements contribute to the meaning of the piece?

After students have completed their Literature Analysis Models individually, they should compare their answers in small groups. These small groups may compile a composite model that includes the ideas of all members. Following the small-group work, teachers have several options for using the models. For instance, they may ask each group to report to the class, they may ask groups to post their composite models, or they may develop a new Literature Analysis Model with the class based on the small-group work. It is important for teachers to hold a whole-group discussion as the final aspect of implementing this model as a teaching-learning device. Teachers are also encouraged to display the selection on a document camera or overhead projector as it is discussed and make appropriate annotations. The teacher should record ideas, underline words listed, and call attention to student responses visually. The teacher should conclude the discussion by asking open-ended follow-up questions. For more information about analyzing literature, see Center for Gifted Education (2011).

Primary Source Document Analysis Model

The Primary Source Document Analysis Model has been developed as a way to teach students:

» how to interpret a historical document,
» how to pose questions to ask about it, and
» how to examine information in the document critically.

The handout (see Figure 4) is designed to assist students as they work through this Primary Source Document Analysis Model. The information that follows includes additional questions and ideas meant to facilitate use of the model. This questions in this model assume the author had an agenda or plan about a specific issue. Thus, it may not be appropriate for use with all primary source documents. For more information about primary sources, see Center for Gifted Education (2007) and Library of Congress (n.d.).

What is the title of the document? Why was it given this title? Students should write the title of the document in this space. The discussion should include probing of why the document was given this title.

What is your reaction to the document? The student will engage with the document and use prior knowledge to make some initial observations and comments. To do that, have students read the document and answer the questions based on their first impressions. You could also revisit the questions on this part of the model after a more thorough analysis of the document has been completed.

When was the document written? Why was it written? The student will focus on the context of the document, as well as its purpose. In order to do that, students must consider the following:

1. Students need to understand the beliefs, norms, and values—the culture—of the period in which the document was developed.
2. Students also need to think about other relevant events and prevalent opinions concerning this issue that were occurring at the time the document was created.
3. Students need to consider the *context*. Additional questions to explore the context could include:
    ○ Who had control of the situation? Who wanted control, but didn't have it?
    ○ Who and what were important to people at this time?
    ○ What did people at this time hope for or value?

HANDOUT

Primary Source Document Analysis Model

Document: _____

What is the title of the document? Why was it given this title?

Title:
Why do you think it was given this title?
Which words in the title are especially important? Why?

What is your reaction to the document?

What is the first thing about this document that draws your attention?
What is in the document that surprises you, or that you didn't expect?
What are some of the powerful ideas expressed in the document?
What feelings does the primary source cause in you?
What questions does it raise for you?

When was the document written? Why was it written?

Who is the author(s)?
When was the document written?
What do you know about the culture of the time period in which the document was written?
What were the important events occurring at the time the document was written?
What was the author's purpose in writing this document?
Who is the intended audience?
What biases do you see in the author's text?

What are the important ideas in this document?

What problems or events does the document address?
What is the author's main point or argument?
What actions or outcomes does the author expect? From whom?
How do you think this author would define _American identity_? What elements of the American identity does the author see as being threatened or cultivated? Why?

What is your evaluation of this document?

Is this document authentic? How do you know?
Is this author a reliable source for addressing this issue/problem?
How representative is this document of the views of the people at this time in history?
How does this document compare with others of the same time period?
What could have been the possible consequences of this document?
What actually happened as a result of this document? Discuss the long-term, short-term, and unintended consequences.
What interpretation of this historical period does this document provide?
How does this document contribute to your understanding of the American identity during this time period?

Figure 4. Primary Source Document Analysis Model.

         ○   Was this issue a new one, an ongoing one, one that was being debated frequently at the time, or one in which few people were interested?

         ○   What were the major events occurring at the time the document was written?

         ○   What were the societal trends occurring at the time this document was written?

4. Once students have determined the context for the document, the next step is to focus on the *purpose* of the document. Additional questions to explore the purpose include:
   ○ Why did the author write this?
   ○ Did a specific event or opinion of the time inspire this document? If so, what was it?
   ○ Did the author have a personal experience that led him or her to write this?
   ○ Did someone require or ask the author to write the document?
   ○ How does the purpose affect the content of the document?

5. Connected to purpose is the *audience*. The same author may write differently for specific groups of people. The primary audience can affect the interpretation of the document.
   ○ For whom was the document created?
   ○ How did the proposed audience affect the content of the document?

What are the important ideas in this document? Once students understand the context and purpose of the document, they will analyze what the document means. Additional questions for probing student understanding of the document's *important ideas* could include:

» What assumptions/values/feelings are reflected in the document?

» What is the author's opinion about the issue?

» Is the author empathetic about the situation, or critical of it?

» Is the author an insider or outsider relative to the issue? Is the author personally involved with the issue or is he or she an observer?

Finally, because the author had a purpose for writing the document, he or she must expect something to happen as a result. These questions can provide additional prompting of student understanding of the *possible results*:

» Who does the author expect to take action in this situation?

» Does the author expect people to change their opinions, to take a specific action, or to consider a new idea?

What is your evaluation of this document? Students will evaluate the document to identify its effectiveness, both for those in the past and for us in the present.

1. The first set of questions focuses on the *authenticity* and *reliability* of a source to help students decide whether or not a document is what it claims or appears to be.
   ○ Authenticity relates to whether the document is real, and not altered or an imitation. Historical documents often have passed through many hands; in doing so, editors or translators may have altered the words or the meaning of the document accidentally or intentionally to reflect their own agendas (Center for Gifted Education, 2007).

○   Reliability relates to the author's qualifications for addressing a given issue or event. In order to write something reliable, authors need to have adequate information and experience with the topic being discussed (Center for Gifted Education, 2007).

Additional questions for discussing the authenticity and reliability of a source are:
○   Could the document have been fabricated, edited, or mistranslated?
○   What evidence do you need to verify the accuracy of the document?
○   What evidence do you have to show that the document was altered at a later time?
○   How reliable is this author?
○   Is the author an authority on this issue, or does he or she have sufficient knowledge to write about it?

2. The second set of questions focuses on how *representative* a document is of views of the time. This requires students to identify the prevalence of the stated ideas in society at the time the document was written.
○   Would many, some, or few people have agreed with the ideas stated in this document?
○   How do the ideas in this document relate to the context of the period in which it was written?
○   How does this document compare with others from the same period? Are there other documents from the time that express similar ideas? Different ideas?
○   What other information might you need to confirm this?

3. The third set of questions relates to considering the *consequences* of a document. First, students must consider the possible outcomes and then the actual ones. By considering the possible outcomes, students can see that multiple options for outcomes existed.
○   What could the possible consequences of this document have been?
○   What might happen if the author's plans were implemented?
○   What could the reaction to the author be when people read this?
○   How might this document affect or change public opinions?
○   What actually happened as a result of this document?
○   How did this document affect people's lives or events at the time (short-term effects)?
○   How did the document affect people at other times in the past, or how does it affect us today (long-term effects)?
○   What were the unintended consequences of this document?

4. The fourth set of questions helps students to determine *how the interpretation informs the reader* about the historical period:
○   What new interpretation of the historical period does this document provide for the reader?
○   How does the document provide an interpretation about the historical period that is not provided through other materials of the time?
○   How does this interpretation inform us about the American identity during this time period?

○ The implementation of this model may be handled similarly to the way in which discussions are held using the Literature Analysis Model: After students have completed their Primary Source Document Analysis Models individually, they should compare their answers in small groups. These small groups may compile a composite model that includes the ideas of all members. Following the small-group work, teachers have several options for using the models, including developing a composite, whole-class model, or posting group models and discussing them. It is important for teachers to hold a group discussion as the final aspect of implementing this model as a teaching-learning device. Teachers are also encouraged to display the selection on a document camera or overhead projector as it is discussed and make appropriate annotations. The teacher should record ideas, underline words listed, and call attention to student responses visually. The teacher should conclude the discussion by asking open-ended follow-up questions.

Music Analysis Model

The Music Analysis Model (see Figure 5) has been developed as a means for teaching students:
» how to interpret lyrics from a song,
» how to pose questions to ask about it, and
» how to examine information in the song critically.

When working with specific songs, encourage students to think critically about both the *lyrics* and *orchestration*, keeping the elements of identity in mind. The Music Analysis Model uses the same key questions as the Primary Source Document Analysis Model, but with wording specifically related to songs:
» What is the title of the song? Why was it given this title?
» What is your reaction to the song?
» When was the song written? Why was it written?
» What are the important ideas in this song?
» What is your evaluation of this song?

As such, many of the same questions listed above for the Primary Source Document Analysis Model may be used for additional probing into student understanding. For additional suggestions about the implementation of this model, please see the note regarding how to manage class discussions after students have completed the Primary Source Document Analysis Model.

Art Analysis Model

The Art Analysis Model (see Figure 6) has been developed as a means for teaching students:
» how to interpret a piece of artwork,
» how to pose questions to ask about it, and
» how to examine the piece of artwork critically.

HANDOUT

Music Analysis Model

Song Title:_____

What is the title of the song? Why was it given this title?

Title:
Why do you think it was given this title?
Which words in the title are especially important? Why?

What is your reaction to the song?

What is the first thing about this song that draws your attention?
What is in the song that surprises you, or that you didn't expect?
What are some of the powerful ideas expressed in the song?
What feelings does the song cause in you?
What questions does it raise for you?

When was the song written? Why was it written?

Who is the songwriter(s)?
When was the song written?
What is the song's purpose? To entertain? To dance to? To critique something?
What were the important events occurring at the time the song was written?
Who is the intended audience?
What biases do you see in the author's lyrics?

What are the important ideas in this song?

Lyrics	Music/Accompaniment
What is the subject of the song? Summarize the song.	Describe the music or melody of this song. Is it fast-paced or slow? Does it have low notes or high notes? Is it melodic or does it have lots of percussion?
What are the main points of the song? What is the song saying about the subject?	What feelings do you get from the music? Why?
What mood/values/feelings does the singer have about the topic?	How does the tone or mood of the music fit with the lyrics? Why might this be?

What is your evaluation of this song?

What new or different interpretation of this historical period does this song provide?
What does this song portray about American identity or how Americans felt at the time?

Figure 5. Music Analysis Model.

HANDOUT

Art Analysis Model

Artist: _____

Artwork/Image: _____

What is the title of the artwork? Why was it given this title?

Title:
Why do you think it was given this title?
Which words in the title are especially important? Why?
What does the title reveal about the artwork?

What do you see in the artwork?

What objects, shapes, or people do you see?
What colors does the artist use? Why?
Are the images in the work realistic or abstract?
What materials does the artist use? Why?

What is your reaction to the image?

What is the first thing about this image that draws your attention?
What is in the image that surprises you, or that you didn't expect?
What are some of the powerful ideas expressed in the image?
What feelings does the image cause in you?
What questions does it raise for you?

When was the image produced? Why was it produced?

Who is the artist?
When was the artwork produced?
What were the important events occurring at the time the artwork was produced?
What was the author's purpose in producing this artwork?
Who is the intended audience?

What are the important ideas in this artwork?

What assumptions/values/feelings are reflected in the artwork?
What are the artist's views about the issue(s)?

What is your evaluation of this artwork?

What new or different interpretation of this historical period does this artwork provide?
What does this artwork portray about American identity or how Americans felt at the time?

Figure 6. Art Analysis Model.

When working with specific pieces of art, encourage students to think critically about both the *image* and the *materials*, keeping the elements of identity in mind. The Art Analysis Model uses many of the same key questions as the Primary Source Document Analysis Model, but with wording specifically related to artwork:

>> What is the title of the artwork? Why was it given this title?
>> What do you see in the artwork?
>> What is your reaction to the image?
>> When was the image produced? Why was it produced?
>> What are the important ideas in this artwork?
>> What is your evaluation of this artwork?

For additional suggestions about the implementation of this model, please see the note regarding how to manage class discussions after students have completed the Primary Source Document Analysis Model.

Summary: Teaching Models

The five teaching models that are included in this unit are essential for facilitating discussions and attaining unit objectives. Teachers should familiarize themselves with these models before beginning the unit and attempt to use them with fidelity. It is important that they use the models repeatedly, as students need practice interacting with the models' components and understanding the questions.

LESSON 1

The Kennedy Years

Alignment of Unit Goals

»   Goal 1: To understand the concept of identity in 1960s America.
»   Goal 2: To develop skills in historical analysis and song and artwork interpretation.
»   Goal 3: To develop analytical and interpretive skills in literature.
»   Goal 4: To develop an understanding of historical events occurring in the United States during the 1960s.

Unit Objectives

»   To describe how changes in American identity in the 1960s are revealed in the music, art, and literature of the decade.
»   To define the context in which a song/piece of art was produced and the implications of context for understanding the artifact.
»   To describe what a selected literary passage means.
»   To describe music, art, and literature of the 1960s that reflected the American identity.

Resources for Unit Implementation

» **Handout 1.1:** Identity Chart
» **Handout 1.2:** Literature Analysis Model
» **Handout 1.3:** Music Analysis Model
» **Handout 1.4:** Music Analysis: British Invasion or Beach Music?
» **Handout 1.5:** Identity Generalizations
» **Handout 1.6:** Pop Art 1960s Unit Project
» **Read:** "Dedication" by Robert Frost (1961). The poem is available at http://www.boston. com/bostonglobe/editorial_opinion/blogs/the_angle/2011/01/frost_at_kenned.html.
» **Listen:** "Camelot" (Lerner & Loewe, 1960) from the *Camelot* soundtrack. The song is available at http://www.youtube.com/watch?v=58mMEJ-kOv0.
» **Read:** Print and Internet resources about the assassination of President John F. Kennedy. Internet resources can be found through a basic Google search.
» **Listen:** The Beatles songs: "Do You Want to Know a Secret" (McCartney & Lennon, 1963a); "I Saw Her Standing There" (McCartney & Lennon, 1963b); "Love Me Do" (McCartney & Lennon, 1963c); and "Twist and Shout" (Medley & Berns, 1961). All songs are available on YouTube.
» **Listen:** The Beach Boys songs: "Surfin'" (Wilson & Love, 1962a); "Surfin' USA" (Wilson & Berry, 1963); "409" (Wilson, Love, & Usher, 1962); and "Surfin' Safari" (Wilson & Love, 1962b). All songs are available on YouTube.

Key Terms

» *Assassination*: the murder of a political figure, often by a surprise attack
» *Identity*: the characteristics by which a person or thing is recognized
» *Camelot*: a popular Broadway musical of the 1960s; it is based on the King Arthur legend.
» Space Race: a competition between the U.S. and the Soviet Union (USSR) for supremacy in space exploration; this was seen as important for national security and symbolic of technological superiority. The Space Race began in 1957 when the USSR launched the first artificial Earth satellite, and continued until 1975.

Learning Experiences

1. Explain to students that during the 1960s, the United States went through economic, political, and cultural changes that changed Americans' perceptions of themselves, of the country, and of their role in the world. In order to understand how these changes affected the average American, students are going to examine the music, literature, and art that was produced and consumed in the U.S. at the time. To see the changes, they first need to review what was going on in America and how Americans viewed themselves and their country at the start of the decade.

2. Students will focus on American identity and how it was changing throughout the 1960s. **Ask:** What is identity? What are the various aspects or parts of someone's identity? Why is a person's identity important? What role does a person's identity play in how he or she acts or what he or she does? Discuss student responses.

3. Distribute the Identity Chart (Handout 1.1) to students and explain to students that some scholars have developed categories of elements that define identity, such as family, race, ethnicity, individuality, beliefs, values, nationality, class, time, and place. They will use this to try to define American identity in 1960. **Ask:**
    a. Time and place: What was our nationality? What were our national symbols and sources of pride? What shared symbols or traditions represented American identity and were seen as meaningful by most Americans?
    b. History and myths: What was the shared background or heritage of the U.S.? What recent events or experiences shaped American views?
    c. Culture and traditions: What was the American idea of family at this time? What were American values in 1960?
    d. Race and ethnicity: What was the status of the races in 1960? What was the role of ethnicity in 1960?
    e. Civic identity: What was the role of the citizen in America? What were our rights and duties as citizens?
    f. International role: What beliefs did America have about itself and others in the world?
    g. Economy: What did the U.S. produce? How did the U.S. generate revenue? What types of jobs did most people have? What was the status of the U.S. economy?

4. Explain to students that they will use the concept of identity as they study the events of the late 20th century and examine the effect of those events on American identity. They will start by looking at the United States in 1960. It was an election year, which John F. Kennedy won. The poet Robert Frost (1961) was asked to read a poem at the inauguration ceremony, and he wrote the poem "Dedication" for that event. On Inauguration Day, Frost couldn't see his notes well and couldn't remember his new poem and ended up reciting an older poem of his. Give students a copy of "Dedication" and a Literature Analysis Model (Handout 1.2) to analyze the poem. **Ask:** What is the mood of the poem? How does he describe the history of the United States? What elements of American identity does he stress in this poem? How does he feel about the future of the United States? Why do you think he feels this way?

5. In his inaugural address, President Kennedy (1961) said, "Let the word go forth from this time and place, to friend and foe alike, that the torch has been passed to a new generation of Americans—born in this century, tempered by war, disciplined by a hard and bitter peace, proud of our ancient heritage . . . " (para. 3) **Ask:** How does this fit with the mood of the Frost poem? How does this match with the identity of Americans in 1960 from your Identity Chart? Explain that President Kennedy's agenda as he started his term was what he called "New Frontiers." He sought to rebuild relations with Latin American countries with his Alliance for Progress, with which the U.S. provided aid to countries that reformed taxes and land policies. He started the Peace Corps, in which young Americans worked in less-developed countries in education, agriculture, and technology. He promised to focus on the Space Race and get a man on the moon by the end of the decade. **Ask:** How were his policies a continuation of what America was doing in the 1950s? How were these goals similar to what was happening in the 1950s? How were his policies a change from the 1950s?

6. Tell students that Kennedy was young, and his wife, Jacqueline Kennedy, was considered a fashion and lifestyle icon. People referred to the Kennedy White House as "Camelot," from a popular Broadway musical of the time. *Camelot* the musical was based on the story of King Arthur and the Knights of the Round Table. Have students listen to "Camelot" (Lerner & Loewe, 1960) and complete a Music Analysis Model (Handout 1.3). **Ask:** What does this song reveal about the ideals or aspirations of Americans in the 1960s? What does it tell us about Americans in the 1960s that they would call Kennedy's White House "Camelot"? Think about the 1960s, and based on what has been happening in the United States, why might people have sought or desired this ideal of Camelot? How would you describe the mood and sentiment of Americans in the year 1960?

7. On November 22, 1963, President Kennedy was assassinated in Dallas, TX, by Lee Harvey Oswald. Have students use print and Internet sources to try to determine the reaction of the American people to Kennedy's death. Conduct a discussion in which students share the resources, which should also include a reaction to the transition of Lyndon B. Johnson into the presidency. **Ask:** How did these events change the mood of Americans in the 1960s? Did Johnson carry on the legacy of the Kennedy administration? (This question could be used as the basis for a debate.)

8. Tell students that in the early 1960s, two music crazes swept the United States: the British invasion and beach music. This gave rise to two music groups that continue to be a part of American musical culture: The Beatles and The Beach Boys. These groups' records went to the top of the charts and were very popular at the time. Give students a Music Analysis: British Invasion or Beach Music? sheet (Handout 1.4). Play the songs from each band that are listed in Resources for Unit Implementation for students and have them analyze the songs. (*Note:* If you play songs not listed under Resources for Unit Implementation, try to focus on the early recordings from each band's debut albums to allow students to analyze the mood of the early 1960s, which will be contrasted with the mood of the late 1960s later on in the unit.)

9. After students have listened to and analyzed the songs, show them the album covers or photos of the two bands from the early 1960s. Photos can be found through a basic Internet search. Again, try to find photos from 1962 or 1963, early in each band's recording careers, for the purpose of the lesson and the unit.

10. Explain to students that they will look at how these forces and others altered American identity using a set of generalizations. Distribute the Identity Generalizations sheet (Handout 1.5) to students and explain that you will work through it together using the Identity Chart (Handout 1.1).

    a. The first generalization is "*Identity changes with new ideas, experiences, conditions or in response to other expressions of identity.*" **Ask:** What new ideas, experiences, or conditions arose during the 1960s? How might these affect American identity?

    b. The second generalization is "*Identity is created, either by a group or person or by outsiders, and self-created identities may be different from how others see one's self.*" **Ask:** How did America see itself in the world? How did the Soviet Union see America? How did the U.S. see China or Southeast Asia? How did these different views shape America's role in the world?

c. The third generalization is *"There are multiple elements of identity and at different times, different elements have greater or lesser importance."* **Ask:** Which elements of identity were most significant in 1960? How has this changed since 1950?

d. The fourth generalization is *"Although members of a group or society may have different individual identities, they still share particular elements of identity."* **Ask:** Despite individual differences, which elements of identity did all Americans have in common?

11. Assign students the unit project, Pop Art in the 1960s (Handout 1.6) to be due at the end of the unit.

Assessing Student Learning

» Identity Chart
» Literature Analysis Model
» Music Analysis activities
» Identity Generalizations
» Discussions

Extending Student Learning

The following are optional activities for extending student learning in this lesson:

» Have students conduct research to find additional information about the Space Race. In a presentation or other format, have the students present their findings to the class.

» Jacqueline Lee Bouvier Kennedy was a First Lady who was loved by the American people for many reasons. Have students develop a timeline of events in her life, including her most important contributions. Students may also want to include information or develop a separate document about her being considered a fashion icon.

» The Kennedy family has a long history of political involvement. Have students develop a chart showing all of the Kennedy family's positions held in local, state, and national government settings.

» Have students research any of the following highlights of the Kennedy administration:
   ○ Cuban Missile Crisis;
   ○ Bay of Pigs initiative;
   ○ Launching of the Peace Corps;
   ○ Civil rights advocacy, sending federal troops to oversee court-ordered integration in Mississippi and Alabama;
   ○ Investment in the U.S. space program;
   ○ Ordering troops into combat in South Vietnam; or
   ○ Signing the limited Nuclear Test Ban Treaty with the United Kingdom and the USSR.

HANDOUT 1.1
Identity Chart

Directions: Complete each box with the elements that define each category of identity.

Identity	
	Time and Place
	Culture and Traditions
	History and Myths
	International Role
	Economy
	Civic Identity
	Race/Ethnicity

Name:_____ Date:_____

HANDOUT 1.2
Literature Analysis Model

Directions: Complete the boxes below to analyze Robert Frost's "Dedication."

Chosen or assigned text: _____	
Key words:	
Important ideas:	
Tone:	
Mood:	
Imagery:	
Symbolism:	
Structure of writing:	

Name:_____ Date: _____

HANDOUT 1.3
Music Analysis Model

Directions: Complete the boxes below after listening to the assigned songs.

Song Title:_____

What is the title of the song? Why was it given this title?

Title:
Why do you think it was given this title?
Which words in the title are especially important? Why?

What is your reaction to the song?

What is the first thing about this song that draws your attention?
What is in the song that surprises you, or that you didn't expect?
What are some of the powerful ideas expressed in the song?
What feelings does the song cause in you?
What questions does it raise for you?

When was the song written? Why was it written?

Who is the songwriter(s)?

Name:_____ Date:_____

When was the song written?
What is the song's purpose? To entertain? To dance to? To critique something?
What were the important events occurring at the time the song was written?
Who is the intended audience?
What biases do you see in the author's lyrics?

What are the important ideas in this song?

Lyrics	Music/Accompaniment
What is the subject of the song? Summarize the song.	Describe the music or melody of this song. Is it fast-paced or slow? Does it have low notes or high notes? Is it melodic or does it have lots of percussion?
What are the main points of the song? What is the song saying about the subject?	What feelings do you get from the music? Why?
What mood/values/feelings does the singer have about the topic?	How does the tone or mood of the music fit with the lyrics? Why might this be?

What is your evaluation of this song?

What new or different interpretation of this historical period does this song provide?
What does this song portray about American identity or how Americans felt at the time?

What does it tell us about Americans in the 1960s that they would call Kennedy's White House "Camelot"? Think about the 1950s; based on what has been happening in the United States, why might people seek or desire this ideal of Camelot?

Name:_____ Date: _____

HANDOUT 1.4
Music Analysis: British Invasion or Beach Music?

Directions: Answer the questions below to compare and contrast the music of The Beatles and The Beach Boys.

What are the songs about?

What images and lifestyle do the songs focus on?

Look at the album covers or other pictures of the two bands. How would you describe the appearances of the bands? How do they fit with the identity of America in the 1960s?

What does the popularity of these songs and this music tell us about the popular mindset of the 1960s?

How are the two bands similar? How are they different?

How would you describe the distinction between British music and beach music?

Why are these two bands and their songs still so popular today?

Name:_____ Date:_____

HANDOUT 1.5
Identity Generalizations

Directions: Use the Identity Chart to explain how each identity generalization below defines the U.S. at the start of the 1960s.

Identity changes with new ideas, experiences, conditions or in response to other expressions of identity.
Identity is created, either by a group or person or by outsiders, and self-created identities may be different from how others see one's self.
There are multiple elements of identity and at different times, different elements have greater or lesser importance
Although members of a group or society may have different individual identities, they still share particular elements of identity

HANDOUT 1.6

Pop Art 1960s Unit Project

One of the defining art styles of the 1960s was Pop Art, and an artist of this style was Andy Warhol. In Warhol's paintings he often had multiple frames of the same image repeated in a grid like at this site: http://www.warhol.org/collection/art/Work/1998-1-138/.

Your task: Based on your understanding of the 1960s, select nine images to include in your grid that demonstrate important or defining events, people, or experiences that shaped American identity or values in the decade.

1. Research and choose the events or people to depict in your images.

2. Create or choose an image or symbol to represent each of your events in your artwork.

3. Write a justification for including these images. You should explain the significance of each event or person in American culture and its importance to American identity in the 1960s.

4. You may include any figures from the decade and you are not restricted to the ones you listened to or read about in the unit. You may expand your research to include authors, music groups, sports figures, political figures, actors, or any other significant individuals from the 1950s.

5. Create a title for your artwork that captures the mood or point of your piece.

6. Put your images together on a poster to display with an artist plaque containing the title, artist, and date.

LESSON 2

The March on Washington and The Civil Rights Movement

Alignment of Unit Goals

> » Goal 1: To understand the concept of identity in 1960s America.
> » Goal 2: To develop skills in historical analysis and song and artwork interpretation.
> » Goal 4: To develop an understanding of historical events occurring in the United States during the 1960s.

Unit Objectives

> » To describe how changes in American identity in the 1960s are revealed in the music, art, and literature of the decade.
> » To define the context in which a song or piece of art was produced and the implications of context for understanding the artifact.

> » To describe a writer's or artist's intent in producing a given song or piece of art based on understanding of text and context.
> » To describe music, art, and literature of the 1960s that reflected the American identity.

Resources for Unit Implementation

> » **Handout 2.1:** Primary Source Document Analysis Model
> » **Handout 2.2:** March on Washington
> » **Handout 2.3:** The Identity of Civil Rights
> » **Read:** "Letter from a Birmingham Jail" by Martin Luther King, Jr. (1963b). The document is available at http://www.africa.upenn.edu/Articles_Gen/Letter_Birmingham.html.
> » **Listen:** "I've Been 'Buked and I've Been Scorned" (1963) by Mahalia Jackson. The performance is available at http://www.cbsnews.com/video/watch/?id=50153816n.
> » **Listen:** "How I Got Over" (Ward, 1951) by Mahalia Jackson. The performance is available at http://www.youtube.com/watch?v=TALcOreZi0A.
> » **Listen:** "Oh Freedom" (n.d) recorded by Joan Baez. A recording of her performance at the March on Washington is not available online, but a different recording from San Francisco is available at http://www.youtube.com/watch?v=PNzmiowUXiQ.
> » **Listen:** "We Shall Overcome" (Tindley, 1947) by Joan Baez. A recording is available at http://www.youtube.com/watch?v=InFwR8G6u2g.
> » **Listen:** "If I Had a Hammer (The Hammer Song)" (Seeger & Hays, 1949) by Peter, Paul and Mary. A recording is available at http://www.youtube.com/watch?v=rBUPr8oDRL8.
> » **Watch:** Martin Luther King, Jr.'s (1963a) "I Have a Dream" speech, available at http://www.youtube.com/watch?v=HRIF4_WzU1w.

Key Terms

> » *Boycott*: to avoid dealing with, purchasing from, or supporting, in order to show lack of support or to intimidate
> » *Civil rights*: rights that protect one's individual freedoms within a society

Learning Experiences

(*Note:* Discussion of the Civil Rights Movement can elicit emotional responses. Teachers should closely monitor the class discussion, especially regarding the derogatory language used to describe different groups of people during this time period.)

1. Tell students that one of the things going on in the 1950s that continued into the 1960s was the growing Civil Rights Movement. **Ask:** What did you study in the 1950s about civil rights? (*Note:* Remind students of Rosa Parks and the Montgomery bus boycott, *Brown v. Board of Education*, and the legal desegregation of schools). Explain to students that the movement continued and expanded in the 1960s. Review in any of the recommended textbooks the events of the early 1960s, such as the lunch counter sit-ins that began in 1960 and the Freedom Riders who challenged bus and station segregation in 1961.

Tell students that the Civil Rights Movement continued to face violence and resistance. One of the most segregated cities in America was Birmingham, AL, where racial bombings and cross burnings led Martin Luther King, Jr. and the Southern Christian Leadership Conference (SCLC) to begin "Project C" ("C" for "confrontation") to integrate the city through a variety of peaceful demonstrations. On Good Friday of April 1963, the SCLC and King led a protest march that resulted in King being put in jail. While in his cell, King wrote his "Letter From a Birmingham Jail." Give students a copy of the letter and have them read and analyze it using the Primary Source Document Analysis Model (Handout 2.1). **Ask:** Martin Luther King, Jr.'s critics said the protests were unwise and untimely. Why do you think they felt this way?

2. Tell students that on August 28, 1963, more than 200,000 people gathered in Washington, DC, for the "March on Washington for Jobs and Freedom." Tell students that they will analyze the songs of this event. Gospel singer Mahalia Jackson sang "I've Been 'Buked and I've Been Scorned" (1963) and "How I Got Over" (Ward, 1951) right before Dr. King spoke. The songs "Oh Freedom" (n.d.) and "We Shall Overcome" (Tindley, 1947) were sung by Joan Baez at the event, and Peter, Paul and Mary sang "If I Had a Hammer (The Hammer Song)" (Seeger & Hays, 1949). Give students a March on Washington sheet (Handout 2.2) to complete as they listen to the songs and read Dr. King's speech. Students can also watch Martin Luther King, Jr. give his "I Have a Dream" speech on YouTube. Discuss student responses.

3. Have the students complete a The Identity of Civil Rights chart (Handout 2.3) to review the content and ideas in this lesson. If you did the civil rights lesson in the 1950s unit, you could compare the two.

4. **Ask:** What was the state of the United States and civil rights in August of 1963? What were the effects of the March on Washington on Americans? The march was attended by celebrities and people of all races. Many of the performers were popular musicians of the time. How might seeing this march on television and seeing the support for the march by prominent diverse people affect American views? Think forward to the political disputes of our current time: How does the support of celebrities affect your feelings about an issue?

Assessing Student Learning

- » Primary Source Document Analysis Model
- » March on Washington activity
- » The Identity of Civil Rights activity
- » Discussions

Extending Student Learning

The following are optional activities for extending student learning in this lesson:
- » Have students work in small groups to research the many movements that grew out of the Civil Rights Movement, such as the women's rights movement, the Puerto Rican movement, the Chicano movement, and the American Indian movement. Each group

should answer these questions: What were the goals of this movement? What did the leaders want to change? Who were some of the leaders of the movement? How was the movement accepted or rejected by the mainstream American society?

» In 2013, the 50th anniversary of the March on Washington was held. Have students research both marches, comparing: speakers, themes and ideas, audience reaction and participation, and other information. Students should include a statement about the extent to which they think that the U.S. had changed or not changed in 50 years regarding civil rights.

HANDOUT 2.1

Primary Source Document
Analysis Model

Directions: Use "Letter From a Birmingham Jail" to compete the chart below.

Document: _____

What is the title of the document? Why was it given this title?

Title:
Why do you think it was given this title?
Which words in the title are especially important? Why?

What is your reaction to the document?

What is the first thing about this document that draws your attention?

Handout 2.1: Primary Source Document Analysis Model, continued

What is in the document that surprises you, or that you didn't expect?
What are some of the powerful ideas expressed in the document?
What feelings does the primary source cause in you?
What questions does it raise for you?

When was the document written? Why was it written?

Who is the author(s)?
When was the document written?

Name:_____ Date:_____

What do you know about the culture of the time period in which the document was written?

What were the important events occurring at the time the document was written?

What was the author's purpose in writing this document?

Who is the intended audience?

What biases do you see in the author's text?

What are the important ideas in this document?

What problems or events does the document address?

Handout 2.1: Primary Source Document Analysis Model, continued

What is the author's main point or argument?
What actions or outcomes does the author expect? From whom?
How do you think this author would define *American identity*? What elements of the American identity does the author see as being threatened or cultivated? Why?

What is your evaluation of this document?

Is this document authentic? How do you know?
Is this author a reliable source for addressing this issue/problem?
How representative is this document of the views of the people at this time in history?

Handout 2.1: Primary Source Document Analysis Model, continued

How does this document compare with others of the same time period?
What could have been the possible consequences of this document?
What actually happened as a result of this document? Discuss the long-term, short-term, and unintended consequences.
What interpretation of this historical period does this document provide?
How does this document contribute to your understanding of the American identity during this time period?

HANDOUT 2.2
March on Washington

Directions: Answer the questions below.

1. Listen to the songs that were sung that day. How do the songs view the future? What is the mood of the songs?

2. What images and allusions do the songs use? Why?

3. Many of these songs were African-American spirituals that had been sung for generations. Why are these songs being sung at this event? What is the significance of these spirituals?

4. Read Martin Luther King, Jr.'s "I Have a Dream" speech.
   a. What is the mood and message of his speech?

   b. What is he asking for in this speech? What does he want to see happen in the United States?

   c. How does he view the future? How likely does he feel that future is?

5. *Although members of a group/society may have different individual identities, they still share particular elements of identity.* How did the feelings and messages of these songs and speeches fit with the identity and views of America in the 1960s? How might the ideas from this march conflict with other views in America? How might the ideas from this event complement or match other views in America at the time? Why?

6. *Identity changes with new ideas, experiences, conditions, or in response to other expressions of identity.* How were the demands and message of the March on Washington different from the views of Civil Rights leaders in the 1950s? (Think back the 1950s with Langston Hughes'"A Dream Deferred" and Nat King Cole's "We Are Americans Too") How were the demands and message in the March similar to the views of the 1950s? What was changing in the United States by 1963? Why?

Name: _____ Date: _____

HANDOUT 2.3

The Identity of Civil Rights

Directions: Use what you've learned in this lesson to answer the questions and complete the chart below.

Identity changes with new ideas, experiences, conditions, or in response to other expressions of identity
What new conditions or identities were African Americans being confronted with during the 1960s?
How did the ideas of the Civil Rights Movement cause Americans as a whole to reexamine or change their own identity? Why?
How did changes in race relations change American identity as a whole?
Why was this change in American identity so difficult for many to accept?
Identity is created, either by a group or person or by outsiders, and self-created identities may be different from how others see one's self.
How did White society view African Americans? What was this perception based on? How were civil rights activists working to change this perception? How did the White-created identity of African Americans shape or explain the different methods or approaches of the Civil Rights Movement?

Although members of a group or society may have different individual identities, they still share particular elements of identity
What elements of identity were shared by both races? What different elements of identity appeared in the 1960s? Why?   What did the different racial identities reveal about America in the 1960s?

LESSON 3

The Motown Sound

Alignment of Unit Goals

- » Goal 1: To understand the concept of identity in 1960s America.
- » Goal 2: To develop skills in historical analysis and song and artwork interpretation.
- » Goal 4: To develop an understanding of historical events occurring in the United States during the 1960s.

Unit Objectives

- » To describe how changes in American identity in the 1960s are revealed in the music, art, and literature of the decade.
- » To describe a writer's or artist's intent in producing a given song or piece of art based on understanding of text and context.
- » To describe major historical events during the 1960s that affected the American identity.
- » To describe music, art, and literature of the 1960s that reflected the American identity.

Resources for Unit Implementation

- » **Handout 3.1:** Music Analysis Model
- » **Handout 3.2:** The Motown Sound
- » **Handout 3.3:** The Revolutionary 1960s
- » **Listen:** "My Girl" (Robinson & White, 1964) by The Temptations. The video is available online at http://www.youtube.com/watch?v=ltRwmgYEUr8.
- » **Listen:** "I Can't Help Myself" (Holland, Dozier, & Holland, 1965a) by Four Tops. The song is available online at http://www.youtube.com/watch?v=qXavZYeXEc0.
- » **Listen:** "Nowhere to Run" (Holland, Dozier, & Holland, 1965b) by Martha and the Vandellas. The song is available online at http://www.youtube.com/watch?v=17yfqxoSTFM.
- » **Listen:** "Stop! In the Name of Love" (Holland, Dozier, & Holland, 1965c) by Diana Ross and The Supremes. The song is available online at http://www.youtube.com/watch?v=iDPjYZxi0n8.
- » **Read:** "A Brief History of Motown" by Gilbert Cruz (2009). The article is available online at http://www.time.com/time/arts/article/0,8599,1870975,00.html#ixzz22bGFItKP.
- » **Listen:** "Tracks of My Tears" (Robinson, Moore, & Tarplin, 1965) by The Miracles. The song is available online at http://www.youtube.com/watch?v=BCwkZrj2VT4.

» **Listen:** "My Guy" (Robinson, 1964) by Mary Wells. The song is available online at http://www.youtube.com/watch?v=r1M5eEJeT38.

Learning Experiences

1. Play segments of "My Girl" (Robinson & White, 1964) and "Stop! In the Name of Love" (Holland, Dozier, & Holland, 1965c). **Ask:** How many of you know these songs? Where have you heard them? What is their role in American culture today?

2. Explain to students that these songs were produced by Motown Records. Review with students "A Brief History of Motown" (Cruz, 2009). **Ask:** How did the Civil Rights Movement make the start of Motown possible? (*Note:* If you have done the 1950s lesson on Elvis and rock and roll, **ask:** What changed since Elvis started his recording career that made Motown possible?)

3. Have students listen to and analyze Motown songs using a Music Analysis Model (Handout 3.1). There are a variety of musicians and songs under Resources for Unit Implementation that you could use for this lesson including Martha and the Vandellas, The Temptations, Four Tops, Diana Ross and the Supremes, Gladys Knight and the Pips, or others mentioned in the *Time* article.

4. Discuss student responses. Show students pictures of these groups from the early to mid-1960s: Martha and the Vandellas, The Temptations, Four Tops, The Miracles, and Diana Ross and the Supremes. Pictures can be found through a basic Internet search. **Ask:** What do you notice about how the groups look? How would you describe the Motown look? How are the way they dress and look similar to the images of the Beatles and the Beach Boys that we looked at earlier? How are they different? Why might this be? Why would Motown producer Berry Gordy create this look for his groups? What does their appearance tell us about American values and attitudes at the time? Have students complete the "The Motown Sound" sheet (Handout 3.2). As a whole class, review student responses.

5. Tell students that Berry Gordy was trying, as the *Time* article points out, to create a product and an identity for his sound. He called Motown Records "Hitsville USA" and promoted it as the "Sound of Young America." **Ask:** Based on what you know about the 1960s, who in America do you think most listened to this music? How might seeing these bands and listening to these records change the perspectives of the listeners about themselves and about the performers? Do you think this music helped change American ideas on race? Why or why not? In what ways?

6. Explain to students that the early 1960s was different from the rest of the decade. The assassination of political leaders, the changing situation in Vietnam, and the changing movement for rights for different groups in the U.S. created change in the 1960s. To examine the effects and nature of those changes, summarize where the U.S. was in during the early fall of 1963 before these changes begin. You may also want to use your textbook to review the major events of the Kennedy era, such as John Glenn orbiting Earth, the launching of the Peace Corps, the Cuban Missile Crisis, and the failed Bay of Pigs invasion. Give students a copy of The Revolutionary 1960s sheet (Handout 3.3) and complete as a class the center box about the U.S. in 1963 based on the information you have been studying.

7. Explain that students will complete the other boxes as they work through the next several lessons. **Ask:** How would you describe the mood of the early 1960s?

Assessing Student Learning

» Music Analysis Model
» The Motown Sound activity
» The Revolutionary 1960s activity
» Discussions

Extending Student Learning

The following are other optional activities for extending student learning in this lesson:

» The Motown Sound was known for its syncopated bass lines, call-and-response choruses, and a strong beat that included tambourines. Although the songs were not political, the popularity of songs coming from Motown contributed to the Civil Rights Movement by achieving crossover success into radio markets that had previously played only music by White artists. Have students conduct additional research about the role of Motown in the Civil Rights Movement: How did Motown contribute in a positive way in the fight for civil rights? What were the downsides to Motown's success? How was founder Berry Gordy's strategy for achieving mainstream success sometimes difficult for the musicians?

» Motown produced many music "icons." Have students define what an "icon" is in this context. Have them determine who the major icons were who were associated with the Motown label. Then, have them determine who modern-day music icons are and make comparisons (music style, music lyrics, clothing, public relations, etc.) to those from the Motown era of the 1960s.

» Have students research popular dances from the 1960s and teach them to their classmates: the Twist, the Jerk, the Swim, the Monkey, the Watusi, the Mashed Potato, the Boogaloo, and the Hitchhiker. (Note to teacher: Instructional videos for many of these dances are available on YouTube. The teacher may want to screen the videos ahead of time for appropriateness.)

Name:_____ Date: _____

Music Analysis Model

Directions: Complete the boxes below after listening to the assigned songs.

Song Title:_____

What is the title of the song? Why was it given this title?

Title:
Why do you think it was given this title?
Which words in the title are especially important? Why?

What is your reaction to the song?

What is the first thing about this song that draws your attention?
What is in the song that surprises you, or that you didn't expect?
What are some of the powerful ideas expressed in the song?
What feelings does the song cause in you?
What questions does it raise for you?

Handout 3.1: Music Analysis Model, continued _____

When was the song written? Why was it written?

Who is the songwriter(s)?	
When was the song written?	
What is the song's purpose? To entertain? To dance to? To critique something?	
What were the important events occurring at the time the song was written?	
Who is the intended audience?	
What biases do you see in the author's lyrics?	

What are the important ideas in this song?

Lyrics	Music/Accompaniment
What is the subject of the song? Summarize the song.	Describe the music or melody of this song. Is it fast-paced or slow? Does it have low notes or high notes? Is it melodic or does it have lots of percussion?
What are the main points of the song? What is the song saying about the subject?	What feelings do you get from the music? Why?
What mood/values/feelings does the singer have about the topic?	How does the tone or mood of the music fit with the lyrics? Why might this be?

What is your evaluation of this song?

What new or different interpretation of this historical period does this song provide?
What does this song portray about American identity or how Americans felt at the time?

Name:_____ Date: _____

HANDOUT 3.2
The Motown Sound

Directions: Complete the Venn diagram and answer the questions below.

1. Compare and contrast Motown music with other popular music of the 1950s and 1960s. In what ways are the three sounds similar? How are they different? Think about the lyrics or topics of the songs, the music, the rhythm, the voice sounds, and the instruments and performance.

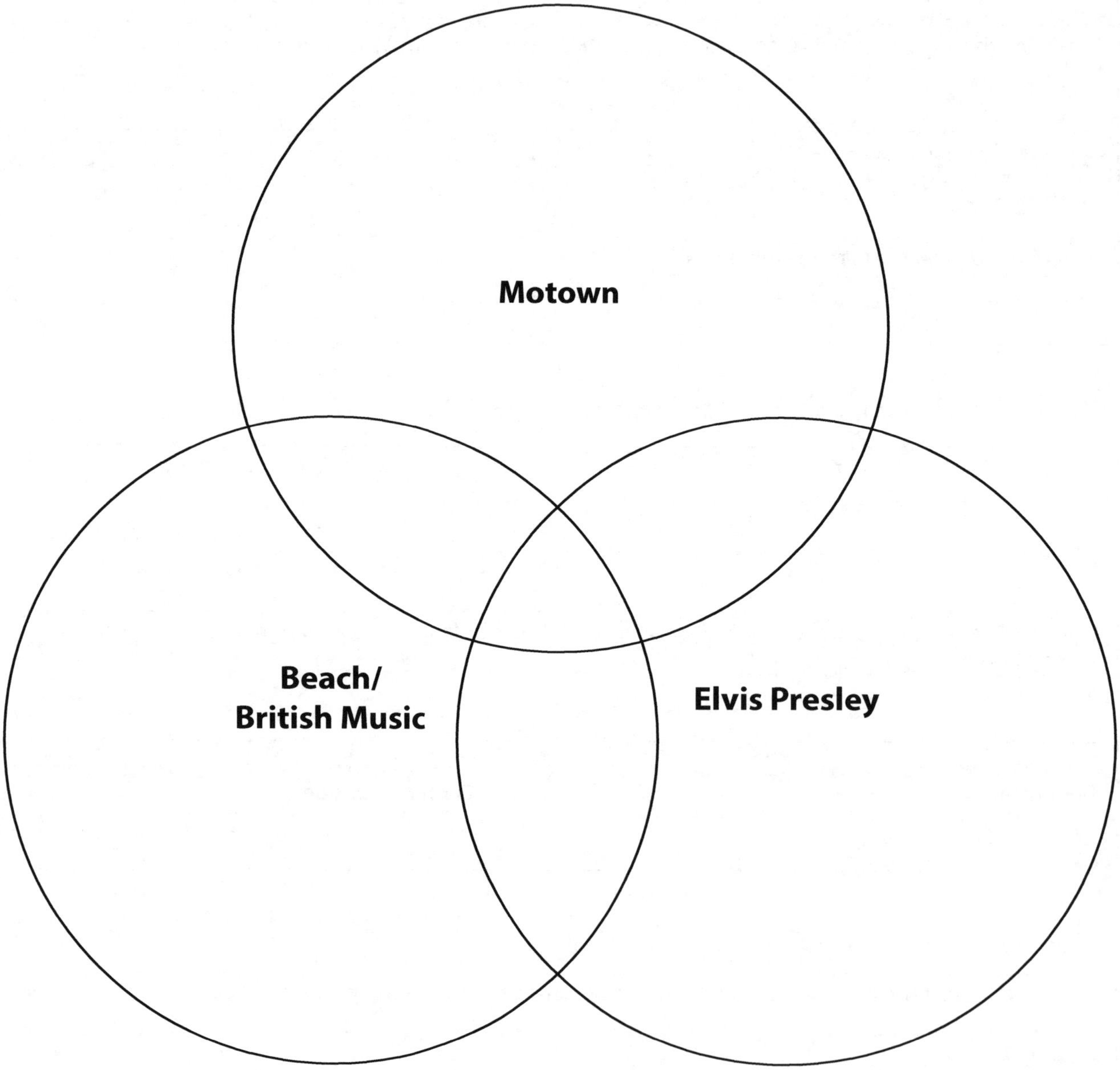

Motown

Beach/ British Music

Elvis Presley

Handout 3.2: The Motown Sound, continued

2. Why do these similarities between the three exist? How might you explain the differences between them? How do these similarities and differences help explain the popularity of Motown music?

3. How did the Motown songs and music fit with what was going on in the Civil Rights Movement? How did Motown support the Civil Rights Movement?

4. How was Motown music different from the music of the Civil Rights Movement? Why might this be? Why was Motown music not specifically talking about civil rights?

5. Why was this music popular with all races? What does that tell us about how American identity was changing by the mid-1960s?

Name: _____   Date: _____

HANDOUT 3.3
The Revolutionary 1960s

Directions: Complete each box as you go over each topic in the unit.

Counterculture	Civil Rights

Culture and Traditions	Race & Ethnicity	International Role
What seem to be American values in 1963? How would you describe life and American society in 1963?	How would you describe racial relations in 1963? How would you describe the experience of different races in 1963?	Describe American interactions with other countries. What is the global status of the U.S.? How do most Americans feel about their role in the world?

What elements of identity seemed to be shared by most people in the United States in 1963?

Environmental Movement	Vietnam	Women's Rights

LESSON 4

Pop Art

Alignment of Unit Goals

» Goal 1: To understand the concept of identity in 1960s America.
» Goal 2: To develop skills in historical analysis and song and artwork interpretation.
» Goal 4: To develop an understanding of historical events occurring in the United States during the 1960s.

Unit Objectives

» To describe how changes in American identity in the 1960s are revealed in the music, art, and literature of the decade.
» To define the context in which a song or piece of art was produced and the implications of context for understanding the artifact.
» To analyze the effects of given documents or artifacts on the interpretation of historical events.
» To describe music, art, and literature of the 1960s that reflected the American identity.

Resources for Unit Implementation

» **Handout 4.1:** Pop Art
» **View:** The following paintings:
   ○ *Campbell's Soup Cans* by Andy Warhol (1962a): Available at http://www.moma.org/collection/object.php?object_id=79809.
   ○ *Twenty-Five Colored Marilyns* by Andy Warhol (1962b): Available at http://www.themodern.org/collection/twenty-five-colored-marilyns/989.
   ○ View: *Brillo Boxes* by Andy Warhol (1964): Available at http://philamuseum.org/collections/permanent/89204.html.
   ○ *F-111* by James Rosenquist (1964–1965): Available at http://www.moma.org/explore/F111.

      ○ *Mr. Bellamy* by Roy Lichtenstein (1961a): Available at http://www.themodern.org/collection/mr-bellamy/917.

      ○ *Washing Machine* by Roy Lichtenstein (1961b): Available at http://www.lichtenstein foundation.org/washmachine.htm.

      ○ *Whaam!* by Roy Lichtenstein (1963): Available at http://www.tate.org.uk/art/artworks/lichtenstein-whaam-t00897.

      ○ *Crying Girl* by Roy Lichtenstein (1964): Available at http://www.lichtenstein foundation.org/3352.htm.

  » **Read:** *The Philosophy of Andy Warhol* (Warhol, 1977). An excerpt is available at http://thephilosophyofandywarhol.blogspot.com/2009/09/6-work.html.

Key Terms

  » *Pop Art:* an art movement that began in the U.S. in the 1960s and reached its peak of activity in the 1960s; the subject matter was everyday icons in American life, such as cartoons, advertisements, packaging, and billboards.

Learning Experiences

1. Display a piece of art by Andy Warhol like *Campbell's Soup Cans*. **Ask:** How many of you have seen pictures like this before? What is your initial reaction to this art? At a quick glance, how would you describe it and the feeling it creates? Explain that this is part of a new school of art called "Pop Art" that emerged in the early 1960s.

2. Give students a Pop Art sheet (Handout 4.1) and show them the artwork listed on the sheet. All of them are available on the Internet. Have students complete the sheet individually as they view the art.

3. As a whole group, **ask:** How would you summarize the subjects of these paintings? If you did not already study Jackson Pollock in the 1950s unit, explain that in the 1950s, Abstract Expressionism shaped art and artists like Jackson Pollock. Show students a Jackson Pollock work if they are unfamiliar with his art. **Ask:** How are subjects of the 1960s paintings different from those in the 1950s? How does the art of the 1960s look different from the 1950s art? How might the trends and events we have been studying explain these differences?

4. **Ask:** What do the appearance and style of the paintings remind you of? Tell students that Lichtenstein and Warhol had been commercial illustrators before turning to painting, Rosenquist had been a sign painter, and both Rosenquist and Warhol had also been window display designers. What had been the purpose of their work before? How did their past work shape their art?

5. **Ask:** What does "pop" mean? Why would this be called "Pop Art"? In what ways does this art fit that definition?

6. **Ask:** What is the purpose or message of this art? Is it simply showing elements or aspects of daily life and popular culture? What are these artists saying about American culture, popular culture, and daily activities? Why does Rosenquist combine all those different

elements in one painting the way he does in *F-111*? What is his statement about American society?

7. Have students individually read "The Philosophy of Andy Warhol" (Warhol, 1977) and discuss together. **Ask:** How does Warhol view life in America? What does he like? What does he criticize? How does this change your interpretation of his art?

8. **Ask:** Think about America in the early 1960s. How does this style of art fit with the music we have been listening to? How does it fit with the mood of the time? What does it tell us about Americans in the 1960s that they were drawn to this type of art and away from the Abstract Expressionism of the 1950s?

Assessing Student Learning

»   Pop Art activity
»   Discussions

Extending Student Learning

The following are optional activities for extending student learning in this lesson:

»   Have each student select an everyday object that represents the current time period. Ask students to transform the objects into their own artwork out of nontraditional material. Before starting, they should make a sketch showing their plans. Have students create the pieces of art, then display them with the titles and explanations of their rationale for choosing the objects, the media used, etc.

»   Roy Lichtenstein's work was characterized by the inclusion of cartoon images, Benday dots, onomatopoeic words, and primary colors. Have students create their own artworks that mimic Lichtenstein's style.

»   Andy Warhol was known for creating many celebrity portraits. Using a technology of their choice, have students create portraits from pictures of their favorite celebrities. (*Note:* If the students actually plan to display the work in a venue other than the classroom, they must seek permission from the photographers to make reproductions of the works and must write to the celebrities or their estates for permission to display the works.)

Name: _____ Date: _____

HANDOUT 4.1
Pop Art

Directions: Complete the chart below by using the paintings you looked at in class.

Title: *Brillo Boxes* by Andy Warhol	Title: *Campbell's Soup Cans* by Andy Warhol
What objects, shapes, or people do you see?	What objects, shapes, or people do you see?
What colors does the artist use?	What colors does the artist use?
Are the images realistic or abstract?	Are the images realistic or abstract?
How does the art make you feel? Why?	How does the art make you feel? Why?
What is the artist's message or statement in this piece of art?	What is the artist's message or statement in this piece of art?
Title: *Twenty-Five Colored Marilyns* by Andy Warhol	**Title: *F-111* by James Rosenquist**
What objects, shapes, or people do you see?	What objects, shapes, or people do you see?
What colors does the artist use?	What colors does the artist use?

Handout 4.1: Pop Art, continued

Are the images realistic or abstract?	Are the images realistic or abstract?
How does the art make you feel? Why?	How does the art make you feel? Why?
What is the artist's message or statement in this piece of art?	What is the artist's message or statement in this piece of art?

Title: *Crying Girl* and *Mr. Bellamy* by Roy Lichtenstein

What objects, shapes, or people do you see?

What colors does the artist use? Why the dots?

Are the images realistic or abstract? What do these images remind you of?

How does the art make you feel? Why?

What is the artist's message or statement in these pieces of art?

Name:_____ Date:_____

Title: *Washing Machine* by Roy Lichtenstein	Title: *Whaam!* by Roy Lichtenstein
What objects, shapes, or people do you see?	What objects, shapes, or people do you see?
What colors does the artist use?	What colors does the artist use?
Are the images realistic or abstract?	Are the images realistic or abstract?
How does the art make you feel? Why?	How does the art make you feel? Why?
What is the artist's message or statement in this piece of art?	What is the artist's message or statement in this piece of art?

In general, how would you summarize the subjects of these paintings?

What traits or aspects of 1960s culture are revealed in these paintings?

What do the appearance and style of the paintings remind you of?

Why would this be called "Pop Art"?

LESSON 5

The 1960s Environmental Movement

Alignment of Unit Goals

- » Goal 1: To understand the concept of identity in 1960s America.
- » Goal 2: To develop skills in historical analysis and song and artwork interpretation.
- » Goal 3: To develop analytical and interpretive skills in literature.
- » Goal 4: To develop an understanding of historical events occurring in the United States during the 1960s.

Unit Objectives

- » To describe how the American identity changed during the 1960s.
- » To describe how changes in American identity in the 1960s are revealed in the music, art, and literature of the decade.
- » To define the context in which a song or piece of art was produced and the implications of context for understanding the artifact.
- » To describe a writer's or artist's intent in producing a given song or piece of art based on understanding of text and context.
- » To consider short- and long-term consequences of a given document or artifact.
- » To describe what a selected literary passage means.
- » To describe major historical events during the 1960s that affected the American identity.

Resources for Unit Implementation

- » **Handout 5.1:** Environmentalism
- » **Handout 5.2:** The American Environment in Song
- » **Handout 5.3:** American Environmental Identity
- » **Handout 3.3:** The Revolutionary 1960s
- » **Read:** Rachel Carson (1962/2002), *Silent Spring*
- » **Read:** Peter Matthiessen (1959/1978), *Wildlife in America*
- » **Read:** Edward Abbey (1968/1985), *Desert Solitaire: A Season in the Wilderness*
- » **Read:** Jack Kerouac (1965/1995), *Desolation Angels*
- » **Listen:** "Little Boxes" by Malvina Reynolds (1962). The song is available online at http://www.youtube.com/watch?v=2_2IGkEU4Xs.
- » **Listen:** "Big Yellow Taxi" by Joni Mitchell (1970). The song is available online at http://www.youtube.com/watch?v=94bdMSCdw20.
- » **Listen:** "Pollution" by Tom Lehrer (1965). The song is available online at http://www.youtube.com/watch?v=nz_-KNNI-no.
- » **Listen:** "Don't Go Near the Water" (Love & Jardine, 1971) by the Beach Boys. The song is available online at http://www.youtube.com/watch?v=7cTIYsvJOQk.

Key Terms

- » *environment*: external factors, such as the air, water, minerals, and organisms, that affect a given organism at any time
- » *preservation*: the process of keeping something safe from harm or injury
- » *suburb*: the area lying right outside a city, usually a residential area

Learning Experiences

1. Explain that many of the things that were going on in the 1950s—the growing suburbs, baby boom, expanding highways, fast food restaurants, and increased prosperity—continued in the early 1960s. **Ask:** What effects did this have on the United States to have more suburbs, more people, and more highways? What new conditions or experiences did this create for Americans? Have students brainstorm a list of the possible consequences (good and bad) of the suburbs, highways, high birthrate, conformity, and popular culture talked about by Andy Warhol.

2. Tell students that by the early 1960s, there was a growing awareness that the changes in lifestyle were starting to affect the natural environment. The book that is seen as the beginning of the environmentalist movement is *Silent Spring* by Rachel Carson (1962/2002), but Peter Mattheison (1959, 1978), Edward Abbey (1968/1985), and other authors were also starting to voice concerns about the effects of American development on the natural landscape. Have students work in groups of four. Have each member of the group read one selection from one of the authors mentioned above and analyze it using the Literature Analysis Model (the first part of Handout 5.1, Environmentalism). Then have each student report to his or her group about the selection and have students complete the Comparison of Works chart (the second part of Handout 5.1, Environmen-

talism). When they have finished in their groups, review their thoughts as a whole group. **Ask:** What are your thoughts on what you read? Do you agree with the author's points of view? Are these new ideas to you? Think about how people in the 1960s, who weren't surrounded by campaigns telling them to recycle, or who had never heard of "going green," would react to reading this. What would they think about these authors and their concerns?

3. Explain to students that these ideas weren't present only in literature, but also in the music of the day. Have students listen to the songs "Little Boxes" by Malvina Reynolds (1962), "Big Yellow Taxi" by Joni Mitchell (1970), "Pollution" by Tom Lehrer (1965), and "Don't Go Near the Water" (Love & Jardine, 1971) by The Beach Boys and complete The American Environment in Song sheet (Handout 5.2) as they listen. After they have responded, discuss as a whole group the student responses. **Ask:** How widespread do you think these concerns were? Do you think many people in the 1960s changed their behaviors and really listened to these songs?

4. Tell students that in 1964, Congress passed the Wilderness Act, which established the National Wilderness Preservation System and set aside 9.1 million acres of wilderness as "forever wild," protected scenic rivers, and expanded the National Parks system. The Water Quality Act of 1964 was passed, setting pollution standards for waterways. Three years later, the Air Quality Act of 1967 tightened standards to diminish air pollution. **Ask:** Why were these laws being passed in the United States? What was changing in America that makes this legislation desired and possible?

5. **Ask:** Which of these environmental issues from the readings or songs do we still face today? Why, after 50 years, do these environmental issues still exist? Why is it so difficult to fix or address these environmental problems? What environmental issues seem to have gotten better over time? Why? What has changed in the last 50 years? How do the attitudes and ideas for solutions in these songs compare to the current movement to "go green"? How is the 1960s environmental movement similar to and different from our current environmental movement? Why?

6. Have students complete the American Environmental Identity Chart (Handout 5.3) in small groups or individually. As a whole class, discuss student responses. **Ask:** What new pressures or ideas did the environmental movement bring to American identity? Put your summary of the effect or influence of the environmental movement into the "Environmental Movement" box of the The Revolutionary 1960s chart (Handout 3.3).

Assessing Student Learning

» Environmentalism activity
» The American Environment In Song activity
» American Environmental Identity activity
» The Revolutionary 1960s activity
» Discussions

Extending Student Learning

The following are optional activities for extending student learning in this lesson:

» Much environmental protection legislation was passed in the 1960s: the Wilderness Act of 1964, the Water Quality Act of 1964, and the Air Quality Act of 1967. Have students research details about the evolution of each piece of legislation, from its passage in Congress to its implementation.

» Many different groups of people became involved in the environmental movement of the 1960s. Have students determine who some of the most influential people and groups were, then have them share the information with classmates with presentation software or a dramatic presentation.

» Ultimately, the environmentalism of the 1960s led to the establishment of Earth Day in 1970. Have students trace specific events leading to the designation of Earth Day. They should also include information about how Earth Day has evolved and is practiced in current times.

HANDOUT 5.1

Environmentalism

Directions: For your selection, complete the following:

Part 1: Literature Analysis Model

Chosen or assigned text:	
Key words:	
Important ideas:	
Tone:	
Mood:	
Imagery:	
Symbolism:	
Structure of writing:	

Name:_____ Date:_____

Part 2: Comparison of Works

Author	What issue is the author discussing?	How does he or she feel about it? What is his or her mood or point of view on the issue?	According to the author, what are Americans doing that causes the issue?	Does the author propose solutions? If so, what? If not, why not?
Rachel Carson, *Silent Spring*				
Peter Matthiessen, *Wildlife in America*				
Edward Abbey, *Desert Solitaire*				
Jack Kerouac, *Desolation Angels*				

What do these authors have in common? How are they different? What does that tell us about the identity or unity of the environmental movement in the 1960s?

HANDOUT 5.2

The American Environment in Song

Directions: Answer the questions below:

Joni Mitchell: "Big Yellow Taxi"

1. What changes in the American landscape are being described?

2. What historical details or trends that we have discussed in class are present in this song?

3. What is the overall mood or point of view of this song? What symbols or images are used to convey this mood? How does the melody and music fit with the mood? Why might this be?

4. What is meant by the phrase, "Don't it always seem to go/That you don't know what you've got/Till it's gone?" Do you think this is true? Why or why not?

5. Do you agree/disagree with the point of view of this song? Why or why not?

Tom Lehrer: "Pollution"

1. What changes in the American landscape are being described in this song?

2. What historical details or trends that we have discussed in class are present in this song?

3. What is the overall mood or point of view of this song? What symbols or images are used to convey this mood?

Handout 5.2: The American Environment in Song, continued

Beach Boys: "Don't Go Near the Water"

1. What changes in the American landscape are being described in this song?

2. What is the overall mood or point of view of this song? What symbols or images are used to convey this mood?

3. Why would a popular music group like The Beach Boys put this song on their latest album?

4. Do you agree/disagree with the point of view of this song? Why?

Malvina Reynolds: "Little Boxes"

1. What changes in the American landscape are being described in this song?

2. What historical details or trends that we have discussed in class are present in this song?

3. What is the overall mood or point of view of this song? What symbols or images are used to convey this mood?

4. What mood do you get from the music or melody of this song? How does the tune fit with the lyrics? Why might this be?

Summary

What similarities exist between the songs?

What changes in the songs do you also see in the U.S. today? Do we see songs like this today? Why or why not?

What changed in the U.S. in the 1960s to make the writers of these songs create them?

HANDOUT 5.3
American Environmental Identity

Directions: Use what you've learned in this lesson to answer the questions below:

There are multiple elements of identity and at different times, different elements have greater or lesser importance.
Why did the environment and our role in the environment become more important in the 1960s? Why was a concern about our effect on the environment not a major part of our identity before the 1960s? What changed to make our concern more prominent in the 1960s?

Although members of a group/society may have different individual identities, they still share particular elements of identity.
Who do you think most supported the environmental movement in the 1960s? How widespread do you think this was? Why? Who might not care or be opposed to the environmental movement? There were many people who were antienvironmentalists; why might this be?

Handout 5.3: American Environmental Identity, continued

**Identity changes with new ideas, experiences, conditions,
or in response to other expressions of identity.**

What new experiences in American life caused Americans to change their perspective on the environment? How did American identity change with regard to its role in the environment?

Is part of American identity based on consumption? Is it part of who we are as a culture to always buy and constantly get newer and better things? Why or why not? What role does consumption and shopping play in American identity in the 1960s? What role does consumption and shopping play in American identity today?

In your opinion, is the environmental movement and the current reduce, reuse, recycle movement changing American views on shopping and buying new things? Why or why not?

LESSON 6

Women in
the 1960s

Alignment of Unit Goals

» Goal 1: To understand the concept of identity in 1960s America.
» Goal 2: To develop skills in historical analysis and song and artwork interpretation.
» Goal 3: To develop analytical and interpretive skills in literature.
» Goal 4: To develop an understanding of historical events occurring in the United States during the 1960s.

Unit Objectives

» To describe how changes in American identity in the 1960s are revealed in the music, art, and literature of the decade.
» To consider short- and long-term consequences of a given document or artifact.
» To describe what a selected literary passage means.
» To make inferences based on information in given passages.
» To describe major historical events during the 1960s that affected the American identity.

Resources for Unit Implementation

»   **Handout 6.1:** *The Feminine Mystique* Questions
»   **Handout 6.2:** Questions: "The National Organization for Women's 1966 Statement of Purpose"
»   **Handout 3.3:** The Revolutionary 1960s
»   **Read:** *The Feminine Mystique* by Betty Friedan (1963/2001). An excerpt available at http://nationalhumanitiescenter.org/ows/seminars/tcentury/FeminineMystique.pdf
»   **Read:** "The National Organization for Women's 1966 Statement of Purpose" by Betty Friedan (1966), available at http://www. now.org/history/purpos66.html

Key Terms

»   *discrimination*: treatment of, or making a distinction in favor of or against, a person based on the group to which the person belongs, rather than on individual merit
»   *gender*: the state of being male or female
»   *mystique*: the aura of mystery surrounding a certain thing or person

Learning Experiences

1. Have students bring in advertisements, comics, or observations that show how gender roles are portrayed. Make two columns on the board, one for "males" and one for "females." **Ask:** What are the roles, behaviors, and attitudes associated with being male in the United States? What are the roles, behaviors, and attitudes associated with being female in the United States? What is the source of these ideas? Why do you answer this way? If we asked this question in another country, would we get the same answers? Explain that gender and gender roles are constructed, meaning they are created by a society and culture over time and are often passed down from one generation to the next. Think about what you learned and what we know about men's jobs and women's jobs in the 1960s. If you made this list in 1960, would it look the same? What would be similar? Different? How are gender roles, and what is accepted for each gender, different now from the 1960s? Explain that part of that change began in the 1960s.

2. Explain to students that when John F. Kennedy became president, one of the things he did was investigate the status of women in the United States. In 1960, women tended to hold lower positions than men in the workplace. There were 17 women serving in Congress, and there were laws that restricted married women's ability to control property or make contracts. President Kennedy authorized a commission, headed by former First Lady Eleanor Roosevelt, to report on differences in employment policies, taxation practices, and legal treatment between men and women, and to provide suggestions for improvement. This report recommended an end to legal discrimination against women and greater equality before the law and in the workplace.

3. **Ask:** What changed in America that would explain why this commission was created at this time? How were American values changing and why?

4. Explain to students that the same year the President's Commission on the Status of Women gave its report, a book by Betty Friedan was published that also talked about

the status of women in the United States. Give students a copy of *The Feminine Mystique* (Friedan, 1963/2001) to read and the questions (Handout 6.1) to answer individually. As a whole class, discuss student responses.

5. Explain that in 1964, the Civil Rights Act was passed, which banned discrimination in public places and outlawed discrimination in employment based on race, religion, national origin, or sex. With the legal support for equal opportunity, women began to push to have this law upheld in practice. In 1966, the National Organization for Women (NOW) was chartered and issued its statement of purpose, written by Betty Friedan (1966). Have students read the excerpts from the NOW charter and answer the questions. **Ask:** How many women in the 1960s do you think agreed with Betty Friedan? What effect do you think this had on American society in the 1960s? Have students respond to Questions: "The National Organization for Women's 1966 Statement of Purpose" (Handout 6.2) and discuss as a group.

6. Have students develop a summary of the influence or effect of the women's movement on American society in the 1960s and put it in the Women's Rights box on the The Revolutionary 1960s sheet (Handout 3.3).

Assessing Student Learning

»   *The Feminine Mystique* Questions
»   Questions: "The National Organization for Women's 1966 Statement of Purpose"
»   The Revolutionary 1960s chart
»   Discussions

Extending Student Learning

The following are optional activities for extending student learning in this lesson:

»   Of course, not all women saw *The Feminine Mystique* in a favorable light. Have students research why the views about women's roles were often extremely divergent in the 1960s.
»   The provision about gender was added late to the Civil Rights Act of 1964 and by some was considered a "fluke." Have students research the development of the wording included in the act and the related controversies.
»   Have students find examples of recent court cases that highlight contemporary concerns about the right to equal opportunities for employment. Have students use the materials as the basis for a discussion about modern concerns about civil rights in the employment arena.

Name:_____ Date: _____

HANDOUT 6.1

The Feminine Mystique
Questions

Directions: Answer the questions below:

1. What is the problem, according to Betty Friedan?

2. She says that "the problem" is hard to define and hard to talk about. Why is that?

3. According to Friedan, what effects are current American gender roles having on women? What effect is there for children?

4. There had been women's rights movements in the 1830s and 1840s and from the turn of the century until the Great Depression. Both movements challenged existing gender roles and the idea that the woman's place was in the home and demanded greater equality for women. Why did this book reignite the women's movement?

5. Who responded favorably to this book? Did all women view this book as positive? Why or why not? What other reactions were there be to this book? Why?

6. How did the ideas in this book challenge or contradict American identity at that time? How did following Friedan's ideas change American society? How did these ideas change gender roles?

7. Looking back at the list of gender roles we started with on the board, have things changed very much from the world Friedan is describing? Are her ideas radical today? How do you react to her writing? Why? Would people in 21st-century America agree with Friedan's views? Why or why not?

HANDOUT 6.2

Questions: "The National Organization for Women's 1966 Statement of Purpose"

Directions: Answer the questions below:

1. What reasons does the document give for changing the status and role of women?

2. What changes does the document say will be required for women to achieve equality?

3. How has technology contributed to changing gender roles?

4. Who is responsible for bringing about the change?

5. Is the argument in this document convincing? Why or why not?

LESSON 7

The Counterculture

Alignment of Unit Goals

» Goal 1: To understand the concept of identity in 1960s America.
» Goal 2: To develop skills in historical analysis and song and artwork interpretation.
» Goal 4: To develop an understanding of historical events occurring in the United States during the 1960s.

Unit Objectives

» To describe how changes in American identity in the 1960s are revealed in the music, art, and literature of the decade.
» To define the context in which a song or piece of art was produced and the implications of context for understanding the artifact.
» To describe a writer's or artist's intent in producing a given song or piece of art based on understanding of text and context.
» To describe major historical events during the 1960s that affected the American identity.

Resources for Unit Implementation

» **Handout 7.1:** Questions: Bob Dylan Lyrics
» **Handout 7.2:** Questions: Jimi Hendrix lyrics
» **Handout 7.3:** Counterculture Identity Chart
» **Handout 3.3:** The Revolutionary 1960s
» **Listen:** Bob Dylan songs, most of which can be found on YouTube:
  ○ "Oxford Town" (Dylan, 1963)
  ○ "North Country Blues" (Dylan, 1964a)
  ○ "With God on Our Side" (Dylan, 1964b)

» **Listen:** Jimi Hendrix songs, all of which can be found on YouTube:
  ○ "1983 . . . (A Merman I Should Turn to Be)" (Hendrix, 1968)
  ○ "Third Stone From the Sun" (Hendrix, 1967)
  ○ "All Along the Watchtower" (Dylan, 1968)

» **Watch:** Jimi Hendrix's rendition of the "Star-Spangled Banner" played at Woodstock, 1969. Footage is available online at http://www.youtube.com/watch?v=wt3cYpFLJiM.

Key Terms

» *counterculture*: the culture and lifestyle of people, often youth, who reject the dominant values of the society in which they live
» *hippie*: a person, especially of the late 1960s, who rejected established institutions and often expressed his or her values externally through casual, folksy clothing
» *lyrics*: the words of a song
» *rendition*: an interpretation of a piece of music

Learning Experiences

1. **Ask:** What is the first thing you think of when you hear "the 1960s"? For most young people, it is "hippies" and Woodstock. **Ask:** What is a hippie? How would you define a hippie? Based on what we have seen so far in the 1960s, what percent of people in the 1960s do you think were actually hippies? Who would most likely be a hippie? Explain that hippies were part of a movement in the U.S. during the 1960s that has come to be known as the "counterculture." The counterculture had a distinct identity within U.S. society that we will look at today.
2. Explain that the reason Woodstock dominates our image of the 1960s was that music and personal expression of values in songs were an important element of the counterculture. In this lesson, students will look at two singers who are symbolic of the counterculture: Bob Dylan and Jimi Hendrix.
3. Give students a lyrics sheet and play the Bob Dylan songs first and have them respond individually to the Questions: Bob Dylan Lyrics sheets (Handout 7.1). Explain that Dylan started recording in the early 1960s and continued throughout the decade into the present. Jimi Hendrix came onto the music scene in 1967 and died in 1970. Hendrix started performing by singing Dylan songs during his musical career. Have students listen to the

Hendrix songs and answer the Questions: Jimi Hendrix Lyrics (Handout 7.2). As a whole group, **ask:** What is similar between the two musicians' songs? How are they different? How do they compare to the Beatles and Beach Boys songs we listened to in Lesson 1? What has changed in the U.S. to cause this change in the music? How does this music compare to the environmental songs from Lesson 5? Do you think the environmental songs were part of the "counterculture"? Why or why not?

4. Give students a Counterculture Identity Chart (Handout 7.3). Have them complete the chart individually or in small groups and then discuss student responses as a whole group.

5. **Ask:** What is the counterculture protesting? Based on its music, how would you define the counterculture and hippies? Play Jimi Hendrix's rendition of the "Star-Spangled Banner" that he played at Woodstock. **Ask:** Does it surprise you that the counterculture is playing the national anthem? What American values did the counterculture still share with the rest of American society? What American values and beliefs are still important to the members of the counterculture? How did the counterculture help shape or counteract the identity of America in the 1960s? Develop a summary of the effect or influence of the counterculture on American identity to put in the Counterculture box of the The Revolutionary 1960s chart (Handout 3.3).

6. **Ask:** Is there similar protest music today? Why or why not? Can you think of any songs that criticize modern culture and seek change? Have students bring in or find songs that critique American society today and have them identify what issue the song is addressing. What is the mood or emotion of the song? What change or action does the song expect? From whom? Have students share their songs and thoughts about them. How is today's protest music similar to the counterculture songs? How is it different? What does this tell us about American society today?

Assessing Student Learning

- » Questions: Bob Dylan Lyrics
- » Questions: Jimi Hendrix Lyrics
- » Counterculture Identity Chart
- » The Revolutionary 1960s chart
- » Discussions

Extending Student Learning

The following are optional activities for extending student learning in this lesson:

- » The hippies were known for their distinctive style of dressing. Have students research the style and prepare a pictorial presentation of their findings.
- » Have students assume the roles of different counterculture groups of the 1960s. Have them present their views in the form of a television documentary hosted by other classmates.
- » Have the students write editorials commenting about whether the effects of the 1960s counterculture were positive or negative. They should include information about communal living, political activism, fashion, sexuality, music, and drugs (depending on the age of the students).

HANDOUT 7.1

Questions: Bob Dylan Lyrics

Directions: Answer the questions below.

"North Country Blues"

1.   What has happened to this town?

2.   According to the narrator of the song, why has this happened? Who is being blamed?

3.   How does this fit with the images of prosperity and middle-class suburbia in the 1960s?

4.   What is Bob Dylan saying about life in America?

"With God on Our Side"

1.   What events in American history are mentioned in this song?

2.   How does the singer say these events were explained to him?

3. What does the singer say about the present events?

4. Does he feel "God is on our side"? What is he saying about American actions and beliefs?

"Oxford Town"

1. Oxford refers to Oxford, MS, where in 1961–1962 an African American man named James Meredith tried to gain entry to the University of Mississippi, but was denied admittance due to his race. President Kennedy ordered U.S. Marshals to protect Meredith when he finally was legally granted admission to the university. The two men who died were a French journalist and a local resident shot by stray bullets in a confrontation between the U.S. Marshals and armed volunteers trying to prevent Meredith from entering the college. Knowing this, what is this song about?

2. How does this song view racial discrimination and the treatment of African Americans in the United States?

3. The fifth stanza says "Somebody better investigate soon." What does that tell you about how the situation is being handled in Oxford, MS?

4. What do you think Dylan means by "Everybody's got their heads bowed down"? Whom does that refer to and why?

Name:_____ Date: _____

HANDOUT 7.2
Questions: Jimi Hendrix Lyrics

Directions: Answer the questions below.

"All Along the Watchtower"

1. Where are the joker and the thief? (fifth stanza)

2. What do they think about this castle they are in? Do they like it?

3. What type of people do they criticize?

4. What do the thief and the joker want?

5. What is this song saying about how the songwriter feels about American society?

"Third Stone From the Sun"

1. How does this song describe Earth?

2. Why doesn't the singer want to go there?

"1983 . . . (A Merman I Should Turn to Be)"

1. What is this song about? What war and fighting is Hendrix referring to?

2. How does Hendirx feel about the fighting? Does he support it? Why or why not?

3. What has Hendrix done to deal with the fighting?

4. What does Hendrix mean by the "killing noise of the out of style"?

HANDOUT 7.3
Counterculture Identity Chart

Directions: Use what you've learned in this essay to answer the questions in each box.

<table>
<tr><td rowspan="6">Identity</td><td>

Culture and Traditions

How do the songs view American popular culture? Which values of popular culture do they criticize? How do they view suburban America? Why? What values do they promote?

</td></tr>
<tr><td>

History and Myths

What historical events or figures does the counterculture mention or allude to? What historical events are important to them?

</td></tr>
<tr><td>

International Role

What do the songs say about the role of the U.S. in the world? What do they want the role of the U.S. to be?

</td></tr>
<tr><td>

Economy

How do the songs view the U.S. economy? Do they see a time of prosperity? What do they criticize?

</td></tr>
<tr><td>

Civic Identity

How do the songs view the role of citizens? What do the songs feel are the responsibilities of citizens?

</td></tr>
<tr><td>

Race/Ethnicity

How do the songs view race? What are their critiques on racial relations in the U.S.?

</td></tr>
</table>

LESSON 8

Protesting the War in Vietnam

Alignment of Unit Goals

- » Goal 1: To understand the concept of identity in 1960s America.
- » Goal 2: To develop skills in historical analysis and song and artwork interpretation.
- » Goal 4: To develop an understanding of historical events occurring in the United States during the 1960s.

Unit Objectives

- » To describe how changes in American identity in the 1960s are revealed in the music, art, and literature of the decade.
- » To define the context in which a song or piece of art was produced and the implications of context for understanding the artifact.
- » To describe a writer's or artist's intent in producing a given song or piece of art based on understanding of text and context.

» To analyze the effects of given documents or artifacts on the interpretation of historical events.

» To describe major historical events during the 1960s that affected the American identity.

» To describe music, art, and literature of the 1960s that reflected the American identity.

Resources for Unit Implementation

» **Handout 8.1:** Music Analysis Model

» **Handout 8.2:** Venn Diagram: War Songs

» **Handout 8.3:** Identity in Time of War

» **Handout 3.3:** The Revolutionary 1960s

» **Listen:** "The Fish Cheer/I-Feel-Like-I'm-Fixin'-to-Die Rag" (McDonald, 1967) by Country Joe and the Fish. The song is available at http://www.youtube.com/watch?v=xsq0SC eQw7s.

» **Listen:** "Lyndon Johnson Told the Nation" by Tom Paxton (1965). The song is available at http://www.youtube.com/watch?v=qTyqoV1d2Ys.

» **Listen:** "Waist Deep in the Big Muddy" by Pete Seeger (1967). The song is available at http://youtube.com/watch?v=j3SysxG6yoE.

» **Listen:** "The Ballad of the Green Berets" (Sadler & Moore, 1966) by Staff Sgt. Barry Sadler. The song is available at http://youtube.com/watch?v=m5WJJVSE_BE.

» **Listen:** "A Hot Time in the Town of Berlin" (De Vries & Buskin, 1944) by Bing Crosby and the Andrews Sisters. The song is available at http://www.youtube.com/watch?v=QrVaObffYNw.

» **Listen:** "Boogie Woogie Bugle Boy" (Ray & Prince, 1941) by the Andrews Sisters. The song is available at http://www.youtube.com/watch?v=qafnJ6mRbgk.

» **Listen:** "Remember Pearl Harbor" (Reid, 1941) by Don Reid and Sammy Kaye. The song is available at http://www.youtube.com/watch?v=_ffJr4Dsm_c.

» **Listen:** "G.I. Blues" (Tepper & Bennett, 1960) by Elvis Presley. The song is available at http://youtube.com/watch?v=JosUZjWUAkQ.

» **Read:** *Beyond Vietnam* by Martin Luther King, Jr. (1967). The text is available at http://www.stanford.edu/group/king/liberation_curriculum/speeches/beyondvietnam.htm.

Key Terms

» *offensive*: an attack, as in warfare

Learning Experiences

1. Using a history textbook, review the U.S. actions in Vietnam through the 1960s up until the Tet Offensive of 1968.

2. Explain to students that they will examine music from the 1960s to analyze how people felt about this war. Give students four copies of the Music Analysis Model (Handout 8.1) and play for students the four Vietnam protest songs. Have students listen and analyze the songs individually. When they have finished, discuss as a whole group. **Ask:** What

stands out to you or surprises you about these songs? What do you notice about the music of the songs? What is the mood of the music? How does that fit with the lyrics? How do these songs portray the war in Vietnam? How do the artists feel about it? How do they describe being a soldier? Who do the artists blame for war and the death of soldiers? Why? Who do they feel is suffering due to the war? How does this view of who is to blame and who is suffering show a divide in the United States? How is the "Ballad of the Green Berets" different from the others?

3. In a whole-group discussion, **ask:** Think back to World War II and World War I: How did Americans respond when we went to war? How do you expect Americans to respond when the U.S. goes to war again? Why?

4. Have students listen to World War II songs and complete the Venn Diagram: War Songs (Handout 8.2) comparing the World War II songs to the Vietnam War songs individually or in a small group. Students should include music, lyrics, mood, view of the war, and view of the life of a soldier in their comparison. Review their responses as a whole group. **Ask:** How do the World War II songs portray the war? How do they express the role of the United States in the war? How are these songs similar to the Vietnam War songs? How are they different? Why do the differences exist? How was the war in Vietnam different from World War II? Why did the U.S. go to war in 1942? How is that different from why the U.S. sent soldiers into Vietnam? How do the different causes of the war explain the different views of the wars in the songs?

5. Explain to students that by 1968, not only were members of the counterculture protesting the war in Vietnam, but other groups and leaders were starting to criticize American involvement in Vietnam. Have students read Martin Luther King, Jr.'s (1967) *Beyond Vietnam* and answer the questions individually. As a group, **ask:** Did you know that Martin Luther King, Jr. spoke out against the war? Does it surprise you? Why or why not? What does he say Vietnam is doing to the United States? Why? Why does he think fighting against the war is part of the fight for civil rights? Who does he feel is suffering because of the war in Vietnam? What does this document tell us about the effect of the Vietnam War on the United States? How many people do you think agreed with him?

6. Explain to students that by 1967, even President Johnson's Secretary of Defense Robert McNamara was beginning to question the U.S. role in Vietnam. In a letter to President Johnson in 1967, McNamara wrote "There may be a limit beyond which many Americans and much of the world will not permit the United States to go. The picture of the world's greatest superpower killing or seriously injuring 1,000 non-combatants a week, while trying to pound a tiny backward nation into submission on an issue whose merits are hotly disputed, is not a pretty one." **Ask:** Hearing this, how many Americans do you think supported the war? What does it tell you that the Secretary of Defense feels this way?

7. Discuss the events of the Tet Offensive of 1968 with students using your textbook. Tell students that in the months before the Tet Offensive, the government had been telling the American people that we were about to win the war, but the success of the Vietnamese during the Tet Offensive proved that the U.S. was not winning at all. **Ask:** How did the American people feel about this? Why? How did this event change American views of the government? How did it change American views of the role of the U.S. in the world?

8. Have students complete an Identity in Time of War chart (Handout 8.3) individually or in a small group. Discuss student responses as a whole group. **Ask:** Think about current

conflicts in the world that the U.S. is involved in. How do people view U.S. troops being in Afghanistan? How do people view the government's decisions about sending troops into other countries? How supportive are the American people of U.S. actions in Afghanistan and other countries? How much criticism have you heard? Did we see widespread criticism of government policies during the wars before Vietnam? How did the Vietnam War and the protest of it change American identity and views of the government and our international role?

9. Develop a summary of the effect of the Vietnam War and protest movement on American identity and society and put it in the Vietnam box on the The Revolutionary 1960s sheet (Handout 3.3).

Assessing Student Learning

- » Music Analysis Model
- » Venn Diagram: War Songs
- » Identity in Time of War activity
- » The Revolutionary 1960s chart
- » Discussions

Extending Student Learning

The following are optional activities for extending student learning in this lesson:

- » One little-known part of the Vietnam story is the role that women played. Have students develop a product that chronicles the story of women in the Vietnam War.
- » Have students research information for a debate between pro- and anti-Vietnam war views.
- » Have students use a talk show format that has several students play key figures from the conflict. As part of the show, the guests would field questions from the audience.
- » Have students prepare a product in which they share information about Vietnam since 1975: art, music, culture, politics, architecture, etc.

Name:_____ Date:_____

HANDOUT 8.1
Music Analysis Model

Directions: Complete the boxes below after listening to the assigned songs.

Song Title:_____

What is the title of the song? Why was it given this title?

Title:
Why do you think it was given this title?
Which words in the title are especially important? Why?

What is your reaction to the song?

What is the first thing about this song that draws your attention?
What is in the song that surprises you, or that you didn't expect?
What are some of the powerful ideas expressed in the song?
What feelings does the song cause in you?
What questions does it raise for you?

Handout 8.1: Music Analysis Model, continued

When was the song written? Why was it written?

Who is the songwriter(s)?
When was the song written?
What is the song's purpose? To entertain? To dance to? To critique something?
What were the important events occurring at the time the song was written?
Who is the intended audience?
What biases do you see in the author's lyrics?

What are the important ideas in this song?

Lyrics	Music/Accompaniment
What is the subject of the song? Summarize the song.	Describe the music or melody of this song. Is it fast-paced or slow? Does it have low notes or high notes? Is it melodic or does it have lots of percussion?
What are the main points of the song? What is the song saying about the subject?	What feelings do you get from the music? Why?
What mood/values/feelings does the singer have about the topic?	How does the tone or mood of the music fit with the lyrics? Why might this be?

What is your evaluation of this song?

What new or different interpretation of this historical period does this song provide?
What does this song portray about American identity or how Americans felt at the time?

HANDOUT 8.2

Venn Diagram: War Songs

Directions: Compare and contrast Vietnam and World War II songs by completing the Venn diagram below.

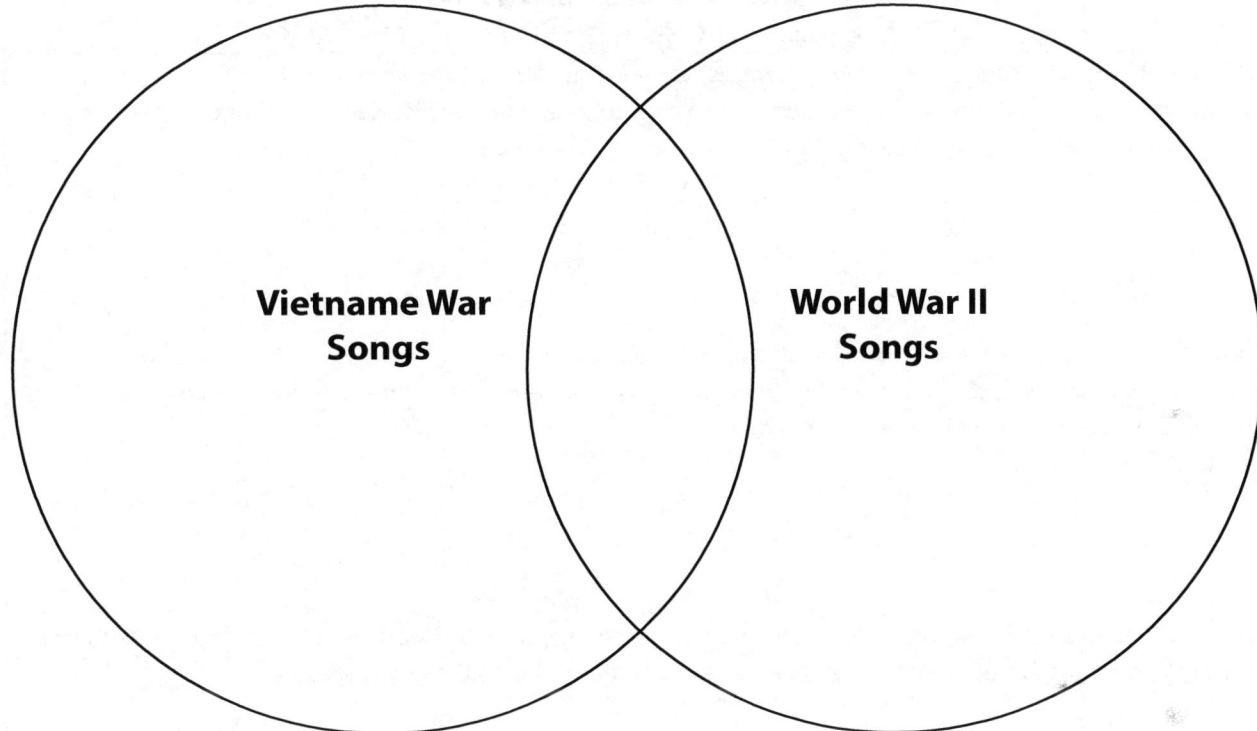

Vietname War Songs

World War II Songs

Name:_____ Date:_____

HANDOUT 8.3
Identity in Time of War

Directions: Use what you've learned in this lesson to complete the chart and answer the questions below.

Identity changes with new ideas, experiences, conditions, or in response to other expressions of identity.
How did American attitudes toward war changed? Do you think Americans were becoming less patriotic? Why or why not? Usually in time of war citizens of a country pull together like we saw in World War II—what happened in the U.S. during Vietnam? Why?
How do the 1960s songs view America's international role? How is this different from how the World War II songs viewed America's role in the world? Why? What has changed? What new experiences or conditions have changed America's view of its international role?
How did American attitudes or views of the government change from the World War II songs to the Vietnam songs? Why might this be? What new experiences or conditions led to these changes?
How did the Vietnam War change American identity? What new traits and beliefs emerged in the U.S.? Why is this?
Although members of a group or society may have different individual identities, they still share particular elements of identity
Do you think all Americans agreed with the views of the Vietnam war songs? Why or why not? Which groups do you think agreed with these songs the most? Are there any ideas or views that might have been shared by most Americans? Why?

LESSON 9

The Civil Rights Movement Changes

Alignment of Unit Goals

» Goal 1: To understand the concept of identity in 1960s America.
» Goal 2: To develop skills in historical analysis and song and artwork interpretation.
» Goal 3: To develop analytical and interpretive skills in literature.
» Goal 4: To develop an understanding of historical events occurring in the United States during the 1960s.

Unit Objectives

» To understand the concept of identity in 1960s America.
» To describe how the American identity changed during the 1960s.
» To describe how changes in American identity in the 1960s are revealed in the music, art, and literature of the decade.
» To develop skills in historical analysis and song and artwork interpretation.
» To define the context in which a song or piece of art was produced and the implications of context for understanding the artifact.
» To develop analytical and interpretive skills in literature.

» To describe what a selected literary passage means.
» To cite similarities and differences in meaning among selected works of literature.
» To make inferences based on information in given passages.
» To develop an understanding of historical events occurring in the United States during the 1960s.
» To describe music, art, and literature of the 1960s that reflected the American identity.

Resources for Unit Implementation

» **Handout 9.1:** Art Analysis Model
» **Handout 9.2:** Literature Analysis Model
» **Handout 9.3:** Black Arts Movement
» **Handout 3.3:** The Revolutionary 1960s
» **View:** "Perceptions of Black" gallery of the Black Arts Movement at http://xroads.virginia.edu/~ug01/hughes/gall.html.
» **Read:** Larry Neal's (1968) description of "The Black Arts Movement." The text is available online at http://nationalhumanitiescenter.org/pds/maai3/community/text8/blackartsmovement.pdf.
» **Read:** Introduction of Don L. Lee's (1969) *Think Black*.
» **Read:** "My Poem" by Nikki Giovanni (1968/2007). The poem is available at http://www.aaregistry.org/poetry/view/my-poem-nikki-giovanni.
» **Read:** "Ka'Ba" by Amiri Baraka (1999). The poem is available at http://www.english.illinois.edu/maps/poets/a_f/baraka/onlinepoems.htm.
» **Read:** "It Is Deep (don't never forget the bridge that you crossed over on)" by Carolyn Rodgers (n.d.). The poem is available at http://english.illinois.edu/maps/poets/m_r/rodgers/online.htm.

Key Terms

» *militancy*: having the willingness to use extreme and sometimes forceful methods to achieve something
» *oppression*: cruelly or unjustly exercising power

Learning Experiences

(*Note:* Discussion of the Civil Rights Movement can elicit emotional responses. Teachers should closely monitor the class discussion, especially regarding the derogatory language used to describe different groups of people during this time period.)

1. Explain to students that by 1965, the Civil Rights Movement was changing. Young people who had been participating in nonviolent protests with the Southern Christian Leadership Conference (SCLC) and the Student Nonviolent Coordinating Committee (SNCC) were unhappy with the lack of progress and started looking for new answers to racial inequality. Using your history textbook as a resource, discuss the ideas of Malcolm X,

Stokely Carmichael, and the Black Panthers. With these new leaders and groups came a new expression of African-American identity in the Black Arts Movement.

2. Have students go to the "Perceptions of Black" gallery of the Black Arts Movement. Allow students to choose one piece of art from each of the five galleries to analyze on the Art Analysis Model (Handout 9.1).

3. After the students have viewed the art, discuss their responses as a whole group **Ask:** In what ways is this art similar to the Pop Art by Warhol and Lichtenstein? How is it different? What is the purpose of this art?

4. Have students read Larry Neal's (1968) description of "The Black Arts Movement." **Ask:** How does he define Black Arts? What is its purpose? How does he feel Black Arts connect to the Black Power movement? He describes the Black Arts as a cultural revolution. What does he mean? What values, views, and beliefs is the Black Arts Movement expressing in American society? How might the Black Arts Movement influence or change American identity and society?

5. Have students read the introduction of Don L. Lee's (1969) *Think Black*. As a whole group, discuss the selection. **Ask:** How does he feel about the art and literature that is currently being produced in the United States? How does he define Black Art? How is the art he is describing different from what you most often see in the U.S.? How do the paintings you looked at fit his definition of Black Art?

6. Regarding the writing of both Neal and Lee, **ask:** How do they define Black Art? How is the art they are describing different from what you most often see in the U.S.? How do the paintings you looked at fit this definition of Black Art?

7. Have students individually or in small groups analyze the three poems listed in Resources for Unit Implementation using the Literature Analysis Model (Handout 9.2). Discuss the messages of the poems together and help students understand them. Explain that Nikki Giovanni's "My Poem" was written in response to criticism she received about earlier poems. **Ask:** How does this help you understand her poem? What is this poem about? What does she mean by "it won't stop the revolution"? Based on what we read by Larry Neal, what is the revolution? What does Amiri Baraka mean by "we labor to make our getaway, into the ancient image; into a new"? How does Amiri Baraka's "Ka'Ba" fit with the ideas of the Black Arts Movement? What is the message of Carolyn Rodgers's poem? What does she mean when she writes, "My mother, religious-negro, proud of having waded through a storm, is very obviously, a sturdy Black bridge that I crossed over, on"? How was her mother's experience different from her own? How is this poem describing the changing status of African Americans in the U.S. by describing the two generations?

8. Give students a "Black Arts Movement" sheet (Handout 9.3) to complete individually or in small groups. Discuss student responses as a whole class. **Ask:** How do these views challenge American identity and society? How is this changing America? Develop a summary of the effect or influence of these changing ideas on American society and put it in the Civil Rights box on the The Revolutionary 1960s sheet (Handout 3.3).

Assessing Student Learning

- » Art Analysis Model
- » Literature Analysis Model
- » Black Arts Movement activity
- » The Revolutionary 1960s activity
- » Discussions

Extending Student Learning

The following are optional activities for extending student learning in this lesson:

- » Have students conduct additional research about the ideas of Malcolm X, Stokely Carmichael, and the Black Panthers. Have them prepare a product in which they compare and contrast their ideas and actions to those of other leaders in the Civil Rights Movement.
- » Although certain names are associated with the Civil Rights Movement, much of what was accomplished was through the efforts of ordinary people at local levels. Have students research the roles of people such as student activists and church leaders. Have them develop a product that is indicative of the people, their strategies, and their accomplishments.

Name: _____ Date: _____

HANDOUT 9.1
Art Analysis Model

Directions: Use the "Preceptions of Black" gallery to answer the questions below.

Gallery 1: Protest and Propaganda

Artist: _____

Artwork/Image: _____

What is the title of the artwork? Why was it given this title?

Title:
Why do you think it was given this title?
Which words in the title are especially important? Why?
What does the title reveal about the artwork?

What do you see in the artwork?

What objects, shapes, or people do you see?
What colors does the artist use? Why?
Are the images in the work realistic or abstract?
What materials does the artist use? Why?

What is your reaction to the image?

What is the first thing about this image that draws your attention?

Handout 9.1: Art Analysis Model, continued

What is in the image that surprises you, or that you didn't expect?
What are some of the powerful ideas expressed in the image?
What feelings does the image cause in you?
What questions does it raise for you?

When was the image produced? Why was it produced?

Who is the artist?
When was the artwork produced?
What were the important events occurring at the time the artwork was produced?
What was the author's purpose in producing this artwork?
Who is the intended audience?

What are the important ideas in this artwork?

What assumptions/values/feelings are reflected in the artwork?
What are the artist's views about the issue(s)?

What is your evaluation of this artwork?

What new or different interpretation of this historical period does this artwork provide?
What does this artwork portray about American identity or how Americans felt at the time?

Name:_____ Date:_____

Gallery 2: Re-presenting the Struggle

Artist: _____

Artwork/Image: _____

What is the title of the artwork? Why was it given this title?

Title:
Why do you think it was given this title?
Which words in the title are especially important? Why?
What does the title reveal about the artwork?

What do you see in the artwork?

What objects, shapes, or people do you see?
What colors does the artist use? Why?
Are the images in the work realistic or abstract?
What materials does the artist use? Why?

What is your reaction to the image?

What is the first thing about this image that draws your attention?
What is in the image that surprises you, or that you didn't expect?

Handout 9.1: Art Analysis Model, continued

What are some of the powerful ideas expressed in the image?
What feelings does the image cause in you?
What questions does it raise for you?

When was the image produced? Why was it produced?

Who is the artist?
When was the artwork produced?
What were the important events occurring at the time the artwork was produced?
What was the author's purpose in producing this artwork?
Who is the intended audience?

What are the important ideas in this artwork?

What assumptions/values/feelings are reflected in the artwork?
What are the artist's views about the issue(s)?

What is your evaluation of this artwork?

What new or different interpretation of this historical period does this artwork provide?
What does this artwork portray about American identity or how Americans felt at the time?

Gallery 3: Self-Determined Black Identity

Artist: _____

Artwork/Image: _____

What is the title of the artwork? Why was it given this title?

Title:
Why do you think it was given this title?
Which words in the title are especially important? Why?
What does the title reveal about the artwork?

What do you see in the artwork?

What objects, shapes, or people do you see?
What colors does the artist use? Why?
Are the images in the work realistic or abstract?
What materials does the artist use? Why?

What is your reaction to the image?

What is the first thing about this image that draws your attention?
What is in the image that surprises you, or that you didn't expect?

Handout 9.1: Art Analysis Model, continued

What are some of the powerful ideas expressed in the image?
What feelings does the image cause in you?
What questions does it raise for you?

When was the image produced? Why was it produced?

Who is the artist?
When was the artwork produced?
What were the important events occurring at the time the artwork was produced?
What was the author's purpose in producing this artwork?
Who is the intended audience?

What are the important ideas in this artwork?

What assumptions/values/feelings are reflected in the artwork?
What are the artist's views about the issue(s)?

What is your evaluation of this artwork?

What new or different interpretation of this historical period does this artwork provide?
What does this artwork portray about American identity or how Americans felt at the time?

Gallery 4: Distinctions of Culture: African Motifs and Musical Beats

Artist: _____

Artwork/Image: _____

What is the title of the artwork? Why was it given this title?

Title:
Why do you think it was given this title?
Which words in the title are especially important? Why?
What does the title reveal about the artwork?

What do you see in the artwork?

What objects, shapes, or people do you see?
What colors does the artist use? Why?
Are the images in the work realistic or abstract?
What materials does the artist use? Why?

What is your reaction to the image?

What is the first thing about this image that draws your attention?
What is in the image that surprises you, or that you didn't expect?

Handout 9.1: Art Analysis Model, continued

| What are some of the powerful ideas expressed in the image? |
| What feelings does the image cause in you? |
| What questions does it raise for you? |

When was the image produced? Why was it produced?

| Who is the artist? |
| When was the artwork produced? |
| What were the important events occurring at the time the artwork was produced? |
| What was the author's purpose in producing this artwork? |
| Who is the intended audience? |

What are the important ideas in this artwork?

| What assumptions/values/feelings are reflected in the artwork? |
| What are the artist's views about the issue(s)? |

What is your evaluation of this artwork?

| What new or different interpretation of this historical period does this artwork provide? |
| What does this artwork portray about American identity or how Americans felt at the time? |

Name:_____ Date:_____

Gallery 5: Mainstream Productions: Black Is a Color

Artist: _____

Artwork/Image: _____

What is the title of the artwork? Why was it given this title?

Title:
Why do you think it was given this title?
Which words in the title are especially important? Why?
What does the title reveal about the artwork?

What do you see in the artwork?

What objects, shapes, or people do you see?
What colors does the artist use? Why?
Are the images in the work realistic or abstract?
What materials does the artist use? Why?

What is your reaction to the image?

What is the first thing about this image that draws your attention?
What is in the image that surprises you, or that you didn't expect?

Handout 9.1: Art Analysis Model, continued

What are some of the powerful ideas expressed in the image?
What feelings does the image cause in you?
What questions does it raise for you?

When was the image produced? Why was it produced?

Who is the artist?
When was the artwork produced?
What were the important events occurring at the time the artwork was produced?
What was the author's purpose in producing this artwork?
Who is the intended audience?

What are the important ideas in this artwork?

What assumptions/values/feelings are reflected in the artwork?
What are the artist's views about the issue(s)?

What is your evaluation of this artwork?

What new or different interpretation of this historical period does this artwork provide?
What does this artwork portray about American identity or how Americans felt at the time?

Name: _____ Date: _____

Literature Analysis Model

Directions: Use the poems you read in class to complete the boxes below.

Chosen or assigned text: _____	
Key words:	
Important ideas:	
Tone:	
Mood:	
Imagery:	
Symbolism:	
Structure of writing:	

HANDOUT 9.3

Black Arts Movement

Directions: Use what you've learned in this lesson to answer the questions below.

Culture and Tradition: What cultures and traditions are important? What values are promoted in this art?

History and Myths: What experiences and events form the past do these authors, artists, and poets focus on? What myths in American culture do they try to end?

Civic Identity: According to these poems, what is the desired civic role for African-Americans? What needs to change?

Economics: How do these works describe the economic condition of African-Americans? How do they seek to change that?

How do the ideas of the art fit the ideas of Martin Luther King Jr.? Malcolm X? Of Stokely Carmichael and Black Power?

Up to this point, what identity or roles has American society created for African-Americans?

How does the Black Arts Movement seek to change this identity? In what ways?

How might White America respond to this art? Why?

What happened in the 1960s that caused and allowed the Black Arts Movement?

LESSON 10

The 1960s Come to an End

Alignment of Unit Goals

   » Goal 1: To understand the concept of identity in 1960s America.
   » Goal 2: To develop skills in historical analysis and song and artwork interpretation.
   » Goal 4: To develop an understanding of historical events occurring in the United States during the 1960s.

Unit Objectives

   » To understand the concept of identity in 1960s America.
   » To describe how the American identity changed during the 1960s.
   » To describe how changes in American identity in the 1960s are revealed in the music, art, and literature of the decade.
   » To define the context in which a song or piece of art was produced and the implications of context for understanding the artifact.

» To describe a writer's or artist's intent in producing a given song or piece of art based on understanding of text and context.
» To develop an understanding of historical events occurring in the United States during the 1960s.
» To describe major historical events during the 1960s that affected the American identity.
» To describe music, art, and literature of the 1960s that reflected the American identity.

Resources for Unit Implementation

» **Handout 10.1:** America in 1967
» **Handout 10.2:** Woodstock
» **Handout 10.3:** America in 1969
» **Handout 3.3:** The Revolutionary 1960s
» **Listen:** "The 59th Street Bridge Song" (Simon, 1967) by Simon and Garfunkel. The song is available at http://www.youtube.com/watch?v=mWBvcJAXwu4.
» **Listen:** "San Francisco" (Phillips, 1967) by Scott McKenzie. The song is available at http://www.youtube.com/watch?v=mJ_WG3d3GL8.
» **Listen:** "Happy Together" (Bonner & Gordon, 1967) by The Turtles. The song is available at http://www.youtube.com/watch?v=mRCe5L1imxg.
» **Listen:** "Yellow Submarine" (Lennon & McCartney, 1966) by The Beatles. The song is available at http://www.youtube.com/watch?v=bM5Nli8m_kQ.
» **Listen:** Playlist from the Woodstock Festival, available at http://www.woodstockstory.com/bandsperformerssetsplaylists1969.html.

Key Terms

» *emergence*: the act of something becoming known
» *assassinate*: to kill someone who is famous or important, usually for political reasons
» *playlist*: a list of songs to be played at a concert or by a radio station

Learning Experiences

1. To review the 1960s, have students present their projects from Lesson 1, the Pop Art 1960s Project.
2. Have students take out the The Revolutionary 1960s sheet (Handout 3.3) that they have been completing after each lesson. Have students complete the America in 1967 sheet (Handout 10.1) using what they have learned in this unit. As a whole group, review student responses and **ask:** Looking at your projects and reflecting about what we have learned about the 1960s, what events and people of the decade have shaped American culture and identity the most? Why do you think this?
3. Explain to students that although they have looked at many groups protesting situations in the U.S., the late 1960s brought the emergence of music that was less politically motivated. In the summer of 1967, approximately 100,000 people gathered in the Haight-Ashbury neighborhood of San Francisco for the "Summer of Love." Similar gath-

erings of young people happened in cities across the United States. Listen to the music of the Summer of 1967 listed in Resources for Unit Implementation. **Ask:** What is the topic of these songs? How do they compare to the music of Dylan or Hendrix? What has changed that might explain these types of songs?

4. Play the Beatles' "Yellow Submarine" (Lennon & McCartney, 1966) and explain that in 1968, the band made an animated film of this song. **Ask:** How has the music of the Beatles changed from what we listened to in Lesson 1? Why might this be? What has been going on throughout the 1960s that might explain their evolution to this type of song?

5. Tell students that after the summer of love in 1967, 1968 brought tension and tragedy. Review the events of 1968. In January, the Tet Offensive proved we weren't winning in Vietnam. In April, Dr. Martin Luther King, Jr. was assassinated. In June, Robert F. Kennedy, seen as the hope for a better future, was assassinated. In August, police and protestors clashed violently at the Democratic National Convention in Chicago. **Ask:** By the end of 1968, how would we describe life in the United States at the close of the 1960s? Is there a clear American identity? How is this different from the U.S. you described on your "America in 1967" sheet? What seems to be the view of the future by the end of 1968?

6. Explain to students that in 1969, things seemed to be looking better. On July 20, Neil Armstrong, an American astronaut, was the first man to walk on the moon, fulfilling John F. Kennedy's pledge to have a man on the moon by the end of the decade. On August 15–17, 1969, thousands gathered for a music festival on a farm near Woodstock, NY. Have students look at the playlist from the Woodstock Festival. **Ask:** Which artists that we have talked about are on this playlist? Which artists aren't on the list that you might expect to see given what we have learned? Why do you expect to see these musicians at Woodstock?

7. Have students individually or in small groups select four to five songs from the Woodstock program from different artists and research their lyrics and listen to them if possible. Have students complete the Woodstock sheet (Handout 10.2).

8. Give students an America in 1969 chart (Handout 10.3) and have students complete it individually or in small groups, drawing upon everything they have learned in the unit. Discuss student responses as a whole class. **Ask:** Look at the America in 1967 sheet completed at the beginning of the lesson. How much has changed in just 2 years? Why is this? What does this tell us about America in the 1960s? What does it suggest about the future of the U.S.?

9. Have students write a journal entry as if they were a teenager living in the 1960s. They should imagine it is December 31, 1969, and they are reflecting back on the decade, the things that have happened, and how they feel about them. They also should include their thoughts on the future: What is their outlook for the new decade? What changes do they anticipate? How do they feel about them, and what is their outlook for the future? Students should try to stay in the mindset of the 1960s.

Assessing Student Learning

» Summative assessment: Unit Project: Pop Arts 1960s
» America in 1967 activity
» Woodstock activity
» America in 1969 activity
» Summative assessment: Journal activity
» Discussions

Extending Student Learning

The following are optional activities for extending student learning in this lesson:

» Have students develop and share oral histories of people who represented some aspect of life in the 1960s: Vietnam veterans, participants in the Civil Right Movement, etc.
» Have students select a musician from the Woodstock playlist to research. Students should prepare a playlist of that artist's music, as well as a written document describing important background information about him or her.

HANDOUT 10.1

America in 1967

Directions: Answer the questions below.

1. What new ideas and experiences were expressed in the U.S. in the 1960s?

2. What new values or priorities were expressed or demanded in the 1960s? How much of a change did these represent for American society?

3. How different are the issues and concerns of the 1960s from the issues and concerns of the U.S. today?

4. Looking at your projects and looking back on what we have learned about the 1960s, what events and people of the 1960s have shaped American culture and identity the most? Why do you think this?

Name:_____ Date: _____

HANDOUT 10.2
Woodstock

Directions: Choose four songs from the Woodstock playlist you went over in class, and answer the questions for each song below.

Song Choice 1:_____

What is the topic of the song?

What feelings or message are in the song?

How does this song reflect the mood and events of the 1960s? What does this song tell us about life in the 1960s?

Describe the group who performs the song:
How many members? Age range? Gender?

How do they dress? How would you describe their appearance?

Song Choice 2:_____

What is the topic of the song?

What feelings or message is in the song?

How does this song reflect the mood and events of the 1960s? What does this song tell us about life in the 1960s?

Describe the group who performs the song:
How many members? Age range? Gender?

How do they dress? How would you describe their appearance?

Handout 10.2: Woodstock, continued

Song Choice 3:_____

What is the topic of the song?

What feelings or message is in the song?

How does this song reflect the mood and events of the 1960s? What does this song tell us about life in the 1960s?

Describe the group who performs the song:

How many members? Age range? Gender?

How do they dress? How would you describe their appearance?

Song Choice 4:_____

What is the topic of the song?

What feelings or message is in the song?

How does this song reflect the mood and events of the 1960s? What does this song tell us about life in the 1960s?

Describe the group who performs the song:
How many members? Age range? Gender?

How do they dress? How would you describe their appearance?

Name:_____ Date:_____

HANDOUT 10.3

America in 1969

Directions: Use what you've learned in this unit to answer the questions below and define American identity at the end of the 1960s.

Identity changes with new ideas, experiences, conditions, or in response to other expressions of identity.
What new ideas, experiences, technology, conditions, or events came about in the 1960s? How did these change American identity—how Americans did things, what they believed and valued? What traits in America were altered? In what ways? What traits went away? What new traits were added? Why? What issues or developments were still being decided at the end of the decade?
There are multiple elements of identity and at different times, different elements have greater or lesser importance
Which elements of identity became more important through the 1960s? Which elements of identity seemed to become less important over the decade?

Handout 10.3: America in 1969, continued

Although members of a group or society may have different individual identities, they still share particular elements of identity
What group identity emerged by the end of the 1960s—what traits did most Americans share? What elements of identity did Americans still have in common? What divisions existed in American society? What challenges or possibilities faced America as a result?

Summarize the 1960s: How would you describe the 1960s? How do you summarize what the decade was all about?

How have the events of the 1960s shaped our modern American identity and culture?

References

Abbey, E. (1985). *Desert solitaire: A season in the wilderness*. New York, NY: Ballantine. (Original work published in 1968)

Baraka, A. (1999). Ka'ba. In *The LeRoi Jones/Amiri Baraka reader* (p. 221). New York, NY: Basic Books.

Bonner, G., & Gordon, A. (1967). Happy together [Recorded by The Turtles]. On *Happy together* [Record]. Los Angeles, CA: White Whale.

Carson, R. (2002). *Silent spring*. New York, NY: Houghton Mifflin. (Original work published 1962)

Center for Gifted Education. (2007). *Guide to teaching social studies curriculum*. Dubuque, IA: Kendall Hunt.

Center for Gifted Education. (2011). *Autobiographies and memoirs*. Dubuque, IA: Kendall Hunt.

Cruz, G. (2009). A brief history of Motown. In *Time*. Retrieved from http://www.content.time.com/time/arts/article/0,8599,1870975,00.html#ixzz22bGFItKP

De Vries, J., & Buskin, J. (1944). A hot time in the town of Berlin [Recorded by Bing Crosby and the Andrews Sisters]. On *(There'll be a) Hot time in the town of Berlin* [Record]. New York, NY: Decca.

Dylan , B. (1963). Oxford town. On *The freewheelin' Bob Dylan* [Record]. New York, NY: Columbia.

Dylan, B. (1964a). North country blues. On *Times they are a-changin'* [Record]. New York, NY: Columbia.

Dylan, B. (1964b). With God on our side. On *Times they are a-changin'* [Record]. New York, NY: Columbia.

Dylan, B. (1968). All along the watchtower [Recorded by Jimi Hendrix]. On *Electric ladyland* [Record]. New York, NY: Reprise.

Friedan, B. (1966). *The National Organization for Women's 1966 statement of purpose*. Retrieved from http://www.now.org/history/purpos66.html

Freidan, B. (2001). *The feminine mystique*. New York, NY: W. W. Norton. (Original work published 1963)

Frost, R. (1961). Dedication. Retrieved from http://www.boston.com/bostonglobe/editorial_opinion/blogs/the_angle/2011/01/frost_at_Kenned.html

Giovanni, N. (2007). My poem. In *The collected poetry of Nikki Giovanni: 1968–1998* (pp. 86–87). New York, NY: Harper Perennial. (Original work published 1968)

Hendrix, J. (1967). Third stone from the sun. On *Are you experienced* [Record]. London, England: Track.

Hendrix, J. (1968). 1983 . . . A merman I should turn to be. On *Electric ladyland* [Record]. New York, NY: Reprise.

Holland, B., Dozier, L., & Holland, E. (1965a). I can't help myself (Sugar pie honey bunch) [Recorded by Four Tops]. On *Four Tops' second album* [Record]. Detroit, MI: Motown.

Holland, B., Dozier, L., & Holland, E. (1965b). Nowhere to run [Recorded by Martha and the Vandellas]. On *Dance party* [Record]. Detroit, MI: Gordy.

Holland, B., Dozier, L., & Holland, E. (1965c). Stop! In the name of love [Recorded by The Supremes]. On *More hits by The Supremes* [Record]. Detroit, MI: Motown.

Huntington, S. P. (2004). *Who are we? The challenges to America's national identity*. New York, NY: Simon and Schuster.

"I've been buked and I've been scorned" [Performed by Mahalia Jackson at the March on Washington, Washington, DC]. (1963). Retreived from http://www.cbsnews.com/video/watch/?id=50153816n

Kennedy, J. F. (1961, January). *Inaugural address*. Speech presented at the inauguration of John F. Kennedy, Washington, DC. Retrieved from http://www.bartleby.com/124/pres56.html

Kerouac, J. (1995). *Desolation angels*. New York, NY: Riverhead. (Original work pubished 1965)

King, M. L., Jr. (1963a). I have a dream. Retrieved from http://www.youtube.com/watch?v=HRIF4_WzU1w

King, M. L., Jr. (1963b). *Letter from a Birmingham jail*. Retrieved from http://www.africa.upenn.edu/Articles_Gen/Letter_Birmingham.html

King, M. L., Jr. (1967, January). *Beyond Vietnam*. Speech presented at Riverside Church, New York, NY. Retrieved from http://www.stanford.edu/group/king/liberation_curriculum/speeches/beyondvietnam.htm

Lee, D. L. (1969). *Think black*. Detroit, MI: Broadside Press.

Lehrer, T. (1965). Pollution. On *Pollution* [Record]. New York, NY: Reprise.

Lennon, J., & McCartney, P. (1966). Yellow submarine [Recorded by The Beatles]. On *Revolver* [Record]. London, England: Parlophone.

Lerner, A., & Loewe, F. (1960). Camelot. On *Camelot: Original Broadway Cast* [CD]. New York, NY: Sony.

Library of Congress. (n.d.). *Using primary sources*. Retrieved from http://www.loc.gov/teachers/usingprimarysources/

Lichtenstein, R. (1961a). *Mr. Bellamy* [Painting]. Retrieved from http://www.themodern.org/collection/mr-bellamy/917

Lichtenstein, R. (1961b). *Washing machine* [Painting].Retrieved from http://www.lichtensteinfoundation.org/wasmachine.htm

Licthenstein, R. (1963). *Whaam!* [Painting]. Retrieved from http://www.tate.org.uk/art/artworks/lichtenstein-whaam-t00897

Lichtenstein, R. (1964). *Crying girl* [Painting]. Retrieved from http://www.lichtensteinfoundation.org/3352.htm

Love, M., & Jardine, A. (1971). Don't go near the water [Recorded by The Beach Boys]. On *Surf's up* [Record]. New York, NY: Reprise.

Matheissen, P. (1978). *Wildlife in America*. New York, NY: Penguin. (Original work published 1959)

McCartney, P., & Lennon, J. (1963a). Do you want to know a secret [Recorded by The Beatles]. On *Please please me* [Record]. London, England: Parlophone.

McCartney, P., & Lennon, J. (1963b). I saw her standing there [Recorded by The Beatles]. On *Please please me* [Record]. London, England: Parlophone.

McCartney, P., & Lennon, J. (1963c). Love me do [Recorded by The Beatles]. On *Please please me* [Record]. London, England: Parlophone.

McKeague, P. M. (2009). *Writing about literature* (9th ed.). Dubuque, IA: Kendall Hunt.

McDonald, J. (1967). The fish cheer/I-feel-like-I'm-fixin'-to-die rag [Recorded by Country Joe and the Fish]. On *I-feel-like-I'm-fixin'-to-die* [Record]. New York, NY: Vanguard.

Medley, P., & Berns, B. (1961). Twist and shout [Recorded by The Beatles]. On *Please please me* [Record]. London, England: Parlophone.

Mitchell, J. (1970). Big yellow taxi. On *Ladies of the canyon* [Record]. New York, NY: Reprise.

National Governors Association Center for Best Practices, & Council of Chief State School Officers. (2010). *Common Core State Standards for English language arts and literacy in history/social studies, science, and technical subjects.* Washington, DC: Authors.

Neal, L. (1968). The black arts movement. *Drama Review, 12*, 29–39.

"Oh, freedom." [Recorded by Joan Baez] (n.d.). On *Joan Baez in San Francisco* [Record]. San Francisco, CA: Fantasy.

Paxton, T. (1965). Lyndon Johnson told the nation. On *Ain't that news!* [Record]. New York, NY: Elektra.

Phillips, J. (1967). San Francisco (be sure to wear flowers in your hair) [Recorded by Scott McKenzie]. On *The voice of Scott McKenzie* [Record]. New York, NY: Columbia.

Ray, D., & Prince, H. (1941). Boogie woogie bugle boy [Recorded by the Andrews Sisters]. On *Buck privates original sound track* [Record]. New York, NY: Universal.

Reid, D. (1941). Remember Pearl Harber [Recorded by Don Reid and Sammy Kay]. On *Remember Pearl Harber* [Record]. New York, NY: Republic.

Reynolds, M. (1962). Little boxes. On *Malvina Reynolds sings the truth* [Record]. Washington, DC: Smithsonian Folkways. (1967)

Robinson, S. (1964). My guy [Recorded by Mary Wells]. On *Mary Wells sings My Guy* [Record]. Detroit, MI: Motown.

Robinson, S., Moore, W., & Tarplin, M. (1965). The tracks of my tears [Recorded by The Miracles]. On *Going to a go-go* [Record]. Detroit, MI: Tamla.

Robinson, S., & White, R. (1964). My girl [Recorded by The Temptations]. On *The Temptations sing Smokey* [Record]. Detroit, MI: Gordy.

Rodgers, C. (n.d.) *It is deep (don't ever forget the bridge that you crossed over on).* Retrieved from http://www.english.illinois.edu/maps/poets/m_r/rodgers/online.html

Rosenquist, J. (1964–1965). *F-111* [Painting]. Retrieved from http://www.moma.org/explore/F111

Sadler, B., & Moore, R. (1966). The ballad of the Green Berets [Recorded by Barry Sadler]. On *Ballads of the Green Berets* [Record]. New York, NY: RCA Victor.

Seeger, P. (1967). Waist deep in the big muddy. [Performed on the *Smothers Brothers Comedy Hour*, February 1968]. Retrieved from http://www.youtube.com/watch?v=j3SysxG6yoE

Seeger, P., & Hays, L. (1949). If I had a hammer (The hammer song) [Recorded by Peter, Paul and Mary]. On *Peter, Paul and Mary* [Record]. Los Angeles, CA: Warner Bros. (1962)

Simon, P. (1967). The 59th Street Bridge song (feelin' groovy) [Recorded by Simon and Garfunkel]. On *Parsley, sage, rosemary, and thyme* [Record]. New York, NY: Columbia.

Smith, A. D. (2010). *National identity (Ethnonationalism comparative perspective).* Malden, MA: Polity Press. Taba, H. (1962). Curriculum development: Theory and practice. New York, NY: Harcourt Brace World.

Tepper, S., & Bennett, R. (1960). G.I. blues [Recorded by Elvis Presley]. On *G.I. blues* [Record]. New York, NY: RCA Victor.

Tindley, C. A. (1947). We shall overcome [Recorded by Joan Baez]. On *We shall overcome* [Record]. Los Angeles, CA: Fontana. (1963)

Ward, C. (1951). How I got over [Performed by Mahalia Jackson at the 1963 March on Washington, Washington DC]. Retrieved from http://www.youtube.com/watch?v=TALcOrezi0A

Warhol, A. (1962a). *Campbell's soup cans* [Painting]. Retrieved from http://www.moma.org/collectioin/object.php?object_id=79809

Warhol, A. (1962b). *Twenty-five colored Marilyn's* [Painting]. Retrieved from http://www. themodern.org/collection/twenty-five-colored-marilyns/989

Warhol, A. (1964). *Brillo boxes* [Painting]. Retrieved from http://philamuseum.org/collections/ permanent/89204.html

Warhol, A. (1977). *The philosophy of Andy Warhol (From A to B and back again)*. New York, NY: Harvest.

Wilson, B., & Barry, C. (1963). Surfin' U.S.A. [Recorded by The Beach Boys]. On *Surfin' U.S.A.* [Record]. Los Angeles, CA: Capitol.

Wilson, B., & Love, M. (1962a). Surfin' [Recorded by The Beach Boys]. On *Surfin' safari* [Record]. Los Angeles, CA: Capitol.

Wilson, B., & Love, M. (1962b). Surfin' safari [Recorded by The Beach Boys]. On *Surfin' safari* [Record]. Los Angeles, CA: Capitol.

Wilson, B., Love, M., & Usher, G. (1962). 409 [Recorded by The Beach Boys]. On *Surfin' safari* [Record]. Los Angeles, CA: Capitol.

APPENDIX

Unit Glossary

assassinate: to kill someone who is famous or important, usually for political reasons

assassination: the murder of a political figure, often by a surprise attack

boycott: to avoid dealing with, purchasing from, or supporting, in order to show lack of support or to intimidate

Camelot: a popular Broadway musical of the 1960s by Lerner and Loewe; it is based on the King Arthur legend.

civil rights: rights that protect one's individual freedoms within a society

counterculture: the culture and lifestyle of people, often youth, who reject the dominant values of the society in which they live

discrimination: treatment of, or making a distinction in favor of or against, a person based on the group to which the person belongs, rather than on individual merit

emergence: the act of something becoming known

environment: external factors, such as the air, water, minerals, and organisms, that affect a given organism at any time

gender: the state of being male or female

hippie: a person, especially of the late 1960s, who rejected established institutions and often expressed his or her values externally through casual, folksy clothing

identity: the characteristics by which a person or thing is recognized

lyrics: the words of a song

militancy: having the willingness to use extreme and sometimes forceful methods to achieve something

mystique: the aura of mystery surrounding a certain thing or person

offensive: an attack, as in warfare

oppression: cruelly or unjustly exercising power

playlist: a list of songs to be played at a concert or by a radio station

Pop Art: an art movement that began in the U.S. in the 1960s and reached its peak of activity in the 1960s; the subject matter was everyday icons in American life, such as cartoons, advertisements, packaging, and billboards

preservation: the process of keeping something safe from harm or injury

rendition: an interpretation of a piece of music

Space Race: a competition between the U.S. and the Soviet Union (USSR) for supremacy in space exploration; this was seen as important for national security and symbolic of technological superiority. The Space Race began in 1957 when the USSR launched the first artificial Earth satellite, and continued until 1975.

suburb: the area lying right outside a city, usually a residential area

# About the Authors

Molly Sandling is a teacher at Jamestown High School in Williamsburg, VA, where she teaches AP U.S. History and AP Human Geography. She completed her master's degree in history at Yale University and her master's degree in education at the College of William & Mary, with an emphasis on adolescent social studies education. While in the master's degree program, she wrote the social studies units *The 1920s in America: A Decade of Tensions, The 1930s in America: Facing Depression, Defining Nations,* and *The Renaissance and Reformation in Europe* and received the NAGC Curriculum Award for *The 1920s in America.* Molly has been teaching since 2000 and was the 2010 High School Teacher of the Year for Williamsburg-James City County Public Schools.

Kimberley Chandler, Ph.D., is the Curriculum Director at the Center for Gifted Education at the College of William and Mary and a clinical assistant professor. Kimberley completed her Ph.D. in Educational Policy, Planning, and Leadership with an emphasis in gifted education adminis-tration at the College of William and Mary. Her professional background includes teaching gifted students in a variety of settings, serving as an administrator of a school district gifted program, and providing professional development training for teachers and administrators nationally and internationally. Currently, Kimberley is the Network Representative on the NAGC Board of Directors, Member-at-Large Representative for the AERA Research on Giftedness and Talent SIG, and editor of the CEC-TAG newsletter *The Update.* Her research interests include curriculum pol-icy and implementation issues in gifted programs, the design and evaluation of professional development programs for teachers of the gifted, and the role of principals in gifted education. Kimberley coauthored a book titled *Effective Curriculum for Underserved Gifted Students* and has served as the editor of many curriculum materials (science, social studies, language arts, and mathematics) from the Center for Gifted Education at The College of William and Mary.

Common Core State Standards Alignment

Grade Levels	Common Core State Standards in ELA-Literacy
K-12 College and Career Readiness Anchor Standards	L.CCRA.R.1: Read closely to determine what the text says explicitly and to make logical inferences from it; cite specific textual evidence when writing or speaking to support conclusions drawn from the text.
	L.CCRA.R.2: Determine central ideas or themes of a text and analyze their development; summarize the key supporting details and ideas.
	L.CCRA.R.4: Interpret words and phrases as they are used in a text, including determining technical, connotative, and figurative meanings, and analyze how specific word choices shape meaning or tone.
	L.CCRA.R.7: Integrate and evaluate content presented in diverse media and formats, including visually and quantitatively, as well as in words.
	L.CCRA.R.9: Analyze how two or more texts address similar themes or topics in order to build knowledge or to compare the approaches the authors take.
	L.CCRA.R.10: Read and comprehend complex literary and informational texts independently and proficiently.